James Bassett

Persia

Eastern mission, a narrative of the founding and fortunes of the Eastern Persia mission, with a sketch of the versions of the Bible and Christian literature in the Persian and Persian-Turkish languages

James Bassett

Persia

Eastern mission, a narrative of the founding and fortunes of the Eastern Persia mission, with a sketch of the versions of the Bible and Christian literature in the Persian and Persian-Turkish languages

ISBN/EAN: 9783337294892

Printed in Europe, USA, Canada, Australia, Japan

Cover: Foto ©Andreas Hilbeck / pixelio.de

More available books at **www.hansebooks.com**

PERSIA:

EASTERN MISSION.

A NARRATIVE

OF THE

FOUNDING AND FORTUNES OF THE EASTERN PERSIA MISSION,

WITH A SKETCH OF THE VERSIONS OF THE BIBLE AND CHRISTIAN LITERATURE IN THE PERSIAN AND PERSIAN-TURKISH LANGUAGES.

BY THE

REV. JAMES BASSETT,

Author of "Persia: Land of the Imams."

PHILADELPHIA:

PRESBYTERIAN BOARD OF PUBLICATION
AND SABBATH-SCHOOL WORK,

1334 CHESTNUT STREET.

COPYRIGHT, 1890, BY

THE TRUSTEES OF THE

PRESBYTERIAN BOARD OF PUBLICATION
AND SABBATH-SCHOOL WORK.

ALL RIGHTS RESERVED.

WESTCOTT & THOMSON,
Stereotypers and Electrotypers, Philada.

TO THE

HONORABLE GEORGE W. BASSETT,

THROUGH WHOSE TENDER AND DEVOTED CARE OF OUR AGED PARENTS THE OPPORTUNITY WAS GIVEN FOR THESE YEARS OF MISSIONARY TOIL,

AND IN

MEMORY OF HIS CONSECRATED LIFE,

THESE PAGES ARE DEDICATED

BY HIS BROTHER,

THE AUTHOR.

PREFACE.

The attention of the public is drawn, at the present time, to Persia by reason of the Shah's recent visit to Europe. It appears to be assumed by many persons that because the people are interested in him they will be concerned to know more of his land and of whatever is likely in any way to affect the future of his kingdom. A glance at what is now commonly written concerning that land will reveal the effort which is made to please the public by presenting whatever is most curious and fabulous in the Shah and his country. When the popular taste for the disgusting cannot be satisfied with fact, there are many writers ready to supply the lack from fancy and to recall the fictions of China and the Middle Ages. When the public taste calls for more refined delusions, the demand is supplied by the suppression of some facts and the exaggeration of others. The people have been taught to look upon the Shah as a coarse beast, or as a magician whose province it is to call up the fabulous era with which the name of Persia has been for so long a time associated. He and his land have been seen through a cloud of romance. His attire and manners, so much in contrast with the costume and ways of European princes, and his sparkling gems, are in keeping with the popular fancy and aid in perpetuating the delusions of past ages. Diplomacy also is busy in magnifying his importance, and rivals vie with one another in inciting the populace to render attentions which may serve to disclose the value of the services which they have given to the Shah, the Queen and the Czar. Amid them all the amiable king of Persia comes as the fabled sheep of the golden fleece, to be either sheared by European sovereigns or to bear back to his own desert country countless aspirations to rival the glory of Christian lands.

In the prevalence of this demand for the fabulous, and while the critics and the people see this far-off country in the magic light of Aladdin's wonderful lamp, I could not reasonably expect to break the spell or meet the call for the graphic and marvelous by the plain story of the humble efforts of a few missionaries. Yet I feel confident of being able to shed a light which, if it does not have the charm to transmute all base things on which it falls to gold and gems, will reveal things as they are, and disclose a power at work in that realm destined to make more useful, if not more mysterious, changes than those which were wrought by Aladdin's lamp. However, if any persons care not to journey with me in my humble way, I leave them to take the "enchanted horse" which stands ready in nearly every bookstall to bear them to the Land of the Sun. I shall have rendered some good service if these pages dispel somewhat of the cloud of fable with which the Shah and his land have been invested, and if they shall cast some light on the conditions in which he is placed. Especially will they serve a good purpose if they shall bring to his aid and to the Christian workers there the sympathies of the friends of progress and the prayers of the Church of God.

The object of this volume is to give the principal facts in the founding and fortunes of the Eastern Persia Mission of the Presbyterian Board of Foreign Missions in the United States. The book, though complete in itself, is part of a more extended one comprehending a narrative of the founding and fortunes of the Church and missions in Persia.

In this volume the author has shunned a repetition of all matters treated of in his earlier work, entitled *Persia: Land of the Imams*, so far as such omission seemed to be consistent with a fair understanding of the subjects considered. For this reason there is in this book no such extended treatment of some topics as their importance might seem to justify. That book describes the natural resources of the country, its principal places, people, customs and religions, and does not give any particular or full account of the missions in that land. But this book treats chiefly of the missionary work.

I think it will be in place here to refer to some errors concerning the missionaries and their work in Eastern Persia which have been bandied about in conspicuous places.

The author of the work entitled *The Land of the Lion and the Sun* in the opening sentence of his book pretends to quote the words of an American missionary. I would remind the readers of that book that the sentence referred to is a falsehood, invented, as I suppose, by Dr. Wills, the author of the work. No American missionary ever used the words given as a quotation in that sentence. Dr. Wills might have found men of his own nation, near at hand, who could say " wall " for *well*, " hegg " for *egg*, and " 'orse " for *horse;* so I can conjecture two reasons only why the doctor should have invented that fiction—namely, to establish the blood-relationship of the American missionaries to himself by pronunciation, or to start off his book on Persia with such a myth as would season all the rest of it.

Many errors of statement are made with reference to the missionary work, both by new missionaries and by those who in America seem to be charged with the duty of providing information for the people. There is altogether too much eagerness on the part of these persons to make their own facts and invest the whole with the charm of romance. I will not attempt to designate all these errors, for many of them have resulted from no evil intent, but simply from lack of knowledge and of disposition to know the facts. But with reference to others it is to be said that it is marvelous how some persons can write words of pious ecstasy with deliberate misrepresentation. Some of these errors will be corrected by the narrative contained in these pages.

It has been my intention to continue the narrative only to the close of the year 1884. Marked changes and progress have been made in Tehran since that date. The mission premises in that city have been sold, and a new site purchased and new buildings erected. But as I have not intimate and personal knowledge of these events, and as the printed reports at command are incomplete, I have not attempted to give any particular account of them.

If what I have written in this little volume shall serve to enlist the interest of those who read it in behalf of the religious welfare of the people of Tehran and Eastern Persia, and lead them to do sincerely what they can for that people, I shall have been repaid for my labor, and shall feel that it has not been lost.

CONTENTS.

CHAPTER I.

Grouping and Names of the Missions—Western and Eastern Missions Defined—Contrasts in the Two Fields—General View of the Country—View from Damavand—Antiquity and Fame of Khorasan—Difference in the People of the Two Divisions—Historical Associations—Great Cities of Persia, Ancient and Modern—Cities of Eastern Persia mentioned in the Bible—People of Eastern Persia—Their Wretched Condition—Houses, Dress and General Appearance—Women and Men—Filthiness of the People—Contrasts . . . . *Page* 23

CHAPTER II.

Intellectual and Religious State of the People—Prominent Features of the Religious State—Persian Mohammedans extremely Religious—Excessive Attention to Externals—The Chief Element of Sheahism—The Divine Right of Ale—Sacredness of the Sayeds—Mohammedan and Protestant Devotions compared—Persian Superstition—Belief in Spirits and Demons: Deves, Jins, Ghouls—Departed Spirits—Faith in Talismans—The Evil Eye—Examples of Demoniacal Possession—Exorcists—Sacred Books possessing Supernatural Power—The Koran in Necromancy—The Armenian Bible—Other Books—Dreams, Faith in; Examples of—Superstition not Confined to the Lower Classes; Examples—

Superstitious Ceremonies—Fears—Spirit of the Religious Orders—Characteristics—Learning Esteemed—Kind of Learning—Love of Religious Discussion—Sinister Motives in Discussion—Ascendency of the Secular Authorities over the Olema—Examples of the Methods of the Mullahs—Cases in Rasht and Ispahan—Controversial Books—Examples of Deception Universal—Deception as an Embellishment of Manners—Fraud the Great Barrier to Progress—Prevalent Vices: Intemperance; Opium-eating; Use of Tobacco; Adultery and Sodomy; Gambling . *Page* 33

CHAPTER III.

Condition of the Women of Persia—Effect of Sheahism on the Popular Estimate of Women—Influence of Fatima—Effect shown by Persian Poetry—Popular Estimate of the Sayeds—Sanctity of Female Sayeds—A Woman's Power over her Husband—Chivalrous Spirit of Persians—Example of the Shah—Reverence of Persians for Maternity—Property Rights of Woman—Conditions Adverse to Woman—Lack of Schools for Females—Child-marriage—Female Seclusion—Woman's Costume—Effect and Prevalence of Polygamy—Baneful Effect of Sekah Marriage—The Non-Mohammedan Women of Persia: Jewesses, Christian Women—Contrasts—Influence of Islam—Degraded Condition of Christian Women—Efforts for the Redemption of Woman in Persia—Proportion of Male and Female Converts—Place Assigned to Women in the Churches—No Converts from Mohammedan Women . . . . *Page* 58

CHAPTER IV.

Particular Account of the Opening of the Mission in Eastern Persia—Appointment of Mr. Bassett to Tehran—Tour of Exploration—Departure of Mr. Bassett and Family from Oroomiah for Tehran—Snowstorm—Incident in a Bulakhanah of Kilishkin—Last Stage of the Journey—Mrs. Bassett . . . . *Page* 74

CONTENTS. 13

CHAPTER V.

Tehran, Situation of—Temperature and Climate—Antiquity of Tehran—Changes in—Later Improvements—Population: Armenians, Jews, Guebers, Mohammedans—Mullahs and Shah—Foreign Legations—State of Society—Mission-Work previous to 1872—Prospective Work of the Missionary—Native Assistants—Religious Toleration—School Opened—Armenian Elders—Baron Matteos—Proposed Union of Schools—Departure of the Shah for Europe—Prime Minister—Shah's Wife—Conspiracy—Erection of a Chapel—Congregation at the Chapel—Opposition of the Archbishop and Elders—Action of the Authorities—Schemes Defeated—Armenians of Feruzbahrom and Zard Aub—Summer Retreat—Vanak—Violence of the Priests—Intemperance of the Villagers—Priest Megerditch—Heat of the Country—Sickness—Increase in Schools—Annual Meeting in Oroomiah—Return to Tehran—Rains and Floods—Persian Houses—The Work in Hamadan—Mechail and Reforms—Priest Oracale—Persecution—Transfer of Native Preachers . . . . *Page* 79

CHAPTER VI.

Persecution in Tabriz—Nestorian Helpers—Tour of Mr. Coan—Petition of Nestorians—How Disposed of—Mr. Bruce in Julfa—Opening of School for Girls—Supply of Books—Proposed Distribution of Scriptures in Khorasan—The City of Yezd—Situation and People—Departure and Tour of Mechail and Babilla—Reception in Yezd—Summoned by the Mujtaheed—Peril—Interposition of the Governor—Flight of the Colporteurs—Results—Transfer of Native Assistants—Opening of School in the Eastern Quarter—Intemperance—Summer Retreat at Tajreesh—Environments—Persian Monogamy—Religious Services—Affairs in Hamadan and Shevarin—Mission Removed to North Side of Tehran, called Shimron Gate—Description of Buildings—Removal of Girls' School—Training-Class—Course of Study—Summary of Schools—Annual Meeting in Tabriz—Arrival of Mr. Potter—Return to Tehran—Work of Mr. Potter—Affairs in Shevarin and Hamadan—Tour to Hamadan—The Governor, Interview with—Trial of the Kathoda—Intemperance of the Native Persian Armenians—The Kashish Khanah—Ceremonies of the Khanah Described—The Khanah Suppressed—Taxes Relevied—Priest Oracale seeks a Remission of the Taxes—Negotiations with the Mustofe—The Priest Presents a Petition to the Shah—Teachers sent to Karaghan and Rasht—Summer Retreat—Ascent of Shimron—Reinforcements—Mr. Bassett's Tour to Tiflis—Rasht, Armenian Congregations in—Sketch of Mission-Work and Results in Rasht—Baku—Armenian Congregation of Protestants—Armenian Priest—Armenians of Shamakha—Sargis, his Work and Character—Detention of Reinforcements—Mission- and Bible-Work in Tiflis—Russian Sabbath—Departure of Missionaries to their Respective Fields—Miss Sarah Bassett takes Charge of the Girls' School—Christian Literature in Persian—Condition of the Persian Scriptures—New Edition of Scriptures Sought—Mr. Wright and the British and Foreign Bible Society—Persian Hymns and Music—Attendance of Jews—Request for Jewish School—Sketch of Jewish School . . . . *Page* 120

CHAPTER VII.

Organization of the Church in Tehran—Need of a Confession—Character of the Converts—Contributions—Hosein Ale, his Parents and Work—Preparation of Mohammedans for the Gospel—Relation of Officers of the Persian Government to Missionaries—The Sadr Azam—Colporteurs in Casveen—Summoned by the Governor—Their Work in the Villages—Hamadan—Changes of Preachers—Arrival of Kasha Shamoon—Sale of Books—Interest among Jews—Narrative of the Work among the Jews—Trials and Aims of the Jews—Firman for their Protection—Their Appeal to the British Society—Changes—Special Services—Publication of the Tract Primer—The Censor of the Press—Testimony of the Mujtaheed concerning the Primer—Other Translations—Mr. Potter's Tour to Mashhade Sar and Quarantine—Route to Mashhade Sar—Work of the New Missionaries—English Services—Statistics of 1878 . . . . *Page* 168

CHAPTER VIII.

Departure of Mr. Potter for America—Departure of Mr. Bassett for Mashhad—Proposed Translation of the Gospel of Matthew—Colporteurs and Books for Mashhad—City and People—Fanatical Character of the Pilgrims and Mullahs—The Jews of Mashhad—Skeptics—Success of the Book-Agents Hosein and Daüd—Sequel of the Work in Mashhad—Book-Dépôt and Colportage—Mirza Daüd—His Work—Return to Tehran—Captive Georgians of Abasabad—Purchase of Premises in Tehran—Titles to Real Estate—Persecution of the Teacher in Karaghan—Supposed Secular Authority of Missionaries—Persecutions in Hamadan—Journey of Mr. Bassett to Hamadan—Visits Karaghan—The Armenian Settlement—Visit of Elders—Preaching—Desecration of the Sabbath—The Priest of Bargoshad—School—Journey by Night—A Village in Need—Appeal for the Sick—Arrival in Hamadan—Visit of the Jews—Their Wants—Jews Baptized—Audience with the Governor—Summer Work—Jews in Tajreesh—Marriage of the Rev. Mr. Potter—His Return to Persia—The Press—New Premises Occupied by the Girls' School—Sickness of Mrs. Scott—Return of Mr. Scott and Family to America—His Death and Character—Persecution of Jews in Hamadan—Orders of Persian Officers—Work in Tehran—Division of Bible-Work—Return of Mr. Bassett to the United States—Sickness by the Way—Work in London—Summary of the Work in Eastern Persia . . . . *Page* 184

CHAPTER IX.

Schools—Marriages—Persecutions in Hamadan—Represented to the British Minister—Yasse Attar—Position of the British Minister—Reasons for—Orders of the Shah touching the Attendance of Mohammedans at the Religious Services and the Instruction of Mohammedans—Attendance Prohibited by the Missionary—Liberty of Non-Mohammedans—Protestant Village—Expediency of forming Christian Villages—Mr. Bruce in Hamadan—Arrival of Mr. Hawkes in Tehran—Bookroom opened in Hamadan—

Death of Agah Jan—Mussulmans Received to the Church—Proposed Occupation of Hamadan—Visit of Missionaries and Mr. Whipple to Hamadan—Work in Hamadan—Division of the Bible-Work in Persia—Report of the year 1880—Girls' School —Persecutions in Hamadan—Persecution of the Pastor—Return of Mr. Bassett and Family—Dr. W. W. Torrence—Voyage on the Caspian—Detention at Ashurada—Journey to Tehran—Changes in the Persian Foreign Office—Flight of Shamoon to Tehran— His Return to Hamadan—Meeting of the Persian Mission— Division of the Mission—Appointment of Mr. Hawkes to Hamadan—Consideration of the Orders of the Persian Government— Copy of the Action taken by the Mission sent to the British Minister—Reply of the Minister—Attendance of Mohammedans— Efforts for a Modification of the Orders—Refusal of the British Minister to Interfere for a Modification—Mission Resolve to Close the Chapel—Appeal to the Persian Foreign Office and to the Shah—Modification granted by the Shah—The Chapel Opened— Two Missions in Hamadan—Mr. Potter Removes to the Western Side of the City—Dr. Torrence opens a Dispensary—Mirza Lazar goes to Rasht—English Services—School for Jews— Nurillah—Boarding-School—Services of Worship and Schools— Miss Bassett Returns to America—Protestant Chapel and Cemetery—Eclipse of the Sun . . . . *Page* 211

CHAPTER X.

Arrival of Reinforcements—Eastern Persian Mission Constituted— Schools—Theodore Isaac—Services of Public Worship in English—Report of the Girls' School for 1882—Book Department— Medical Department—The Native Church—Death of Usta Abraham—Erection of a New Chapel—The Building Described— Opposition excited by the Amene Sultan—Attempt to Purchase the Mission-Premises by the Amene—The Work in Hamadan— Persecutions—Mirza Sayed Khan—Beginning of the Mission of the United States to Persia—Inquiries concerning the Safety of Citizens of the United States in Persia—Report of the British Foreign Office in Reply—First Appointment under the Act of

Congress—Appointment of S. G. W. Benjamin—His Arrival in Persia—His Antecedents and Qualifications—Public Worship in English—Services in Persian—Matters with the Amene Sultan—Affairs in Hamadan—The Secretary of the Legation goes to Hamadan—Attempts of the Old Armenians in Hamadan—Persecutions—Pleasant Episodes—Miss S. Bassett returns to Persia in Company with Miss Sherwood—Summary of the Year's Work—Work for Women, as shown by the Reports of Mrs. Bassett and Mrs. Potter—A Glimpse of the Girls' School, as given by the Report of Miss Bartlett—Special Religious Interest in the Winter of 1883–84—Summer Residence and Work—Resignation and Return of Mr. Bassett to America; Reasons therefor—Statements of the Annual Report—Summary of the Year's Work in Hamadan—Summary of Statistics of the Mission—Miss Schenck's Quarterly Report—Miss Bassett's Report of the Year's Work in the Girls' School . . . . *Page* 238

CHAPTER XI.

Methods of Mission-Labor in Persia, especially Eastern Persia—Methods Modified by the Condition of the People—The Romantic Method—Finding a Congregation—Henry Martyn's Experience—Street-Preaching not Attempted in Mohammedan Villages—Practicable in Christian Villages—Obstacles to Gathering Congregations—Intolerance of Islam—Opposition of the Priests—Too Sensitive a Conscience—Time-honored Religions—Protestantism too Honest—Power and Futility of Controversy—Other Methods Essential—Interested and Disinterested Motives—Desire for Education and Power of Schools—Permanent Congregations, how Formed—Difficulty in the Way of Obtaining Native Preachers—Nestorian Preachers—Armenians of Eastern Persia—Assistants to be Trained—Religious Services—Persians accustomed to Public Worship—Habits of Reverence—Preaching—Music—Influence of Sacred Song—The Organ—Matter of Preaching—Doctrines of Religion—Objectionable Doctrines—The Ale Allahees—Effect of the Peculiarities of the Persian Religion on the Relations of Persians to Christianity—Imitation of Christian

Doctrine, and Assumptions—Resemblance to Rome—Revulsion from Rome—Conflict of the Gospel and Sheahism—Method of Successful Approach—Preparatory Instruction of Converts—Circulation of the Scriptures—Instances of the Influence of the Bible—The Circulation of Other Books—Pfander's Works—Books in the Armenian Language—Kind of Books Needed—Use of Medical Missions—Special Efforts for Persian Women by Christian Women . . . . *Page* 281

CHAPTER XII.

Difficulties Peculiar to the Field—Expensive Establishments—Display of Wealth—Educational Establishments—Similarity of Motives in Tehran and in New York—Missionaries are Representatives—Impression Created by Foreign Legations—Criticism of Missionaries—Requirements in the Way of Schools—Judicious Use of Funds—Espionage of the Persian Authorities—Preoccupation of the Minds of the People by Worldly Allurements—Usual Influence of Foreigners—Demand for Foreign Protection—Advantages of the Field—A Centre of Influence for the Kingdom—Political Influences—Persian Young Men—Good Influence of Foreigners—Consecration of Wealth . . . . . . *Page* 301

CHAPTER XIII.

Difficulties and Encouragements in the Whole Field—Intolerance—Peculiarities of Persian Mohammedanism—The Weaker Phase—The Difficulty of the Mental Condition—Policy of European Governments—Dispersed State of the Non-Mohammedan People—Encouragements—Increase of Intelligence, Means of: Telegraphs, Postal System—Favorable Impression of Foreigners—Results of Missionary Work—Precedents in Favor of Religious Liberty—Success of Bible-Work—Exploration—Preparatory Work—Present and Prospective Effect of the Russian Advance on the Eastern Border of Persia—Natural Resources of Eastern Persia—Elements of Change—Policy of European Nations . . . . *Page* 315

CONTENTS. 19

CHAPTER XIV.

Providential Calls—Power of Social Influences—Plea for Some Isolated Communities—Abasabad Georgians—Jews of Mashhad—A College in Tehran, Reasons for . . . . *Page* 326

CHAPTER XV.

The Bible in Persia—No Evidence of Christian Literature in Persian in Early Times—The Bible First in Importance—First Version of any Part of the Bible in Persian—Version of Tus—Version of Kaffa—Version of Wheeloc and Pierson—Earlier Conjectured Version—Version of Nadir Shah—Version of Col. Colbrook—Version of L. Sebastiani—Version of Henry Martyn—Version of the Psalter by Henry Martyn—Dates of Publication of Different Editions—Glen's Version of the Psalms—Poetical and Prophetical Books—Version of the Historical Books by Pinkerton and Lee—Publication of Glen's Version of the Psalms and Proverbs—Glen's Version of the Old Testament, printed at Edinburgh—Robinson's Version of the Old Testament—Version of the Psalms by Mirza Abraham—Calcutta Edition of Martyn's Version—Lithograph Edition of Robinson's Version—Bruce's Version—Versions in Turkish—Amirchanjanz's Version in Transcaucasian Tartar—Publication of the Transcaucasian Version—Labaree's Version in Azarbijanee—Bassett's Version in Turkmanee—Difficulties in the Way of Translating in Persian—Great Size of the Volume of the Persian Bible—New Edition in Small Size—Lodiana Edition—Efforts in the Way of the Circulation of the Scriptures in Persia—Favorable Attitude of the Persian Government toward Christian Literature—Other Religious Books in Persian—By Whom and When Made—Books in Persian Turkish . . . . *Page* 331

ILLUSTRATIONS.

	PAGE
MULLAHS	45
SHAH OF PERSIA	61
ARMENIAN WOMEN	69
TEHRAN FROM THE ISPAHAN ROAD	81
JEWS OF TEHRAN	87
BURIAL-TOWER AND PLAINS OF RA AND TEHRAN	91
GUEBERS' BURIAL-TOWER	95
PRIME MINISTER IN COURT COSTUME	103
MECHAIL AND HIS WIFE	117
APARTMENTS OF THE KING'S TREASURER	129
GIRLS' SCHOOL, TEHRAN	133
TRAINING-CLASS OF YOUNG MEN	137
GOVERNOR OF ARDELAN	141
ARMENIAN PRIEST	145
ARMENIAN PATRIARCH	149
BAKU	157
BAKU MUSSULMAN AND WIFE	161
SHRINE OF REZA	185
DERVISH	189
MISSION-PREMISES, TEHRAN	205
INTERIOR OF NEW CHAPEL	243
HUT AND BOOTH NEAR RASHT	253
ARMENIAN MOTHER AND SON	257
CAREPET AND HIS WIFE VICTORIA	263
BRITISH LEGATION	305

PERSIA: EASTERN MISSION.

CHAPTER I.

Grouping and Names of the Missions—Western and Eastern Missions Defined—Contrasts in the Two Fields—General View of the Country—View from Damavand—Antiquity and Fame of Khorasan—Difference in the People of the Two Divisions—Historical Associations—Great Cities of Persia, Ancient and Modern—Cities of Eastern Persia mentioned in the Bible—People of Eastern Persia—Their Wretched Condition—Houses, Dress and General Appearance—Women and Men—Filthiness of the People—Contrasts.

THE missions of the Presbyterian Board of Foreign Missions in Persia are grouped under two names—"The Western Persia Mission" and "the Eastern Persia Mission." The terms denote the position of the two divisions with relation to one another, and not an exact and equal division of the area of the country with reference to the points of the compass. If it were required to divide the land in length from east to west on the thirty-sixth parallel by a line drawn from north to south, the latter line would intersect the former at or very near Mount Damavand, or about forty miles east of Tehran.

The provinces of Khorasan and Karman comprise Eastern Persia, geographically considered. But as the greater part of these provinces is an uninhabited desert, the capital may be considered as practically the central city of the eastern section. It is really the geographical centre of the northern part of the country only, or of that part lying north of the thirty-third parallel. The missions of the "Board" above named have no station or work south of that latitude. All their operations have been carried on, therefore, in what is properly called Northern Persia, except such incidental effort as may have been made south of the city of Hamadan. The cities of Casveen and Senah are the most western towns in which work has been, or is likely to be, done by the missionaries of Tehran and Hamadan, and the regions east of the former places constitute the field of the Eastern Persia Mission.

This section of the country differs in some particulars from the district west of it. The greatest differences are in the extent of desert, altitude of mountains and plains, and in the races of people and their languages. The western part is a country of high table-lands, the centre of the kingdom. Here the plains are from four to six thousand feet above the sea, and the mountains called Zagros cover the southern portion of this field. In the north the Elburz Mountains form a striking contrast with the great desert stretching southward and eastward at their base. They differ from the mountains of Western

Persia in their great altitude and in their general direction. Several peaks in this range rise to a height of from twelve to fifteen thousand feet above the sea, and Damavand, the loftiest mountain of Western Asia, marks very nearly the centre of the range in its stretch across the kingdom from the western shore of the Caspian Sea to the eastern border, and stands as a sentinel looking over the wide desolation of the great desert on the south and on the waters of the Caspian Sea on the north. If there is a marked contrast in the contour of the mountains and plains of the two divisions we have made, there is but little difference in the aspects of barrenness and desolation, for these appearances belong to all Persia, excepting only the narrow strips of forest along the shores of the sea and the few verdant fields which here and there greet the eye, and which are small oases in a broad expanse of arid plains.

The view which the traveler obtains as he ascends some high mountain in that country is a fair index of the aspect of all the interior. He sees mountain separated from mountain by broad plains in monotonous succession, and all destitute of verdure and glaring in the fierce rays of an unclouded sun. But the plains are not wholly without objects of interest. Some of them are covered with flowers of many bright colors, among which the poppy is most conspicuous, and the air is laden with the sweet odor of the camel-thorn and other shrubs. Could the traveler climb the side of Mount

Damavand, and could his eye take in the entire prospect presented from the summit of that mountain, he would see the strange contrast between the aspect of the regions of the interior and those of the Caspian coast— the contrast between desert and dense forest, between a cloudy sky, an arid and clear air and thick vapors rising above the sea and forest as from a boiling caldron. As one looks out upon the dreary scene, the wide uninhabited spaces, and perceives no traces of great towns and great works of the past ages, it is difficult to believe that here some of the chief cities of antiquity flourished and these plains resounded to the tread and shout of mighty armies.

The greater part of Eastern Persia is included within the large province of Khorasan, a name which means the "Land of the Sun," and which has often been applied to the whole kingdom. It is a country which, though so widely desert, is more celebrated in Persian poetry and romance than any other part of the land. It rivals in the great deeds of its people all other provinces of the realm. Here are laid the principal scenes of the mythical era. Here the great heroes of the fabulous period first became known to fame. Here the Aryans first made their homes in Persia. Here the great Parthian kingdom was born. Here the first successful revolt against Arab rule in Western Asia was devised, and hence was propagated the greatest schism of the Mohammedan world.

The western and eastern sections of the country differ in races of people and in their speech. In the west the inhabitants are for the most part of either the Turkish or the Kurdish race. In the east, however, the Aryan and pure Persian stocks prevail, and the Persian tongue is the language most commonly used.

The central districts of this eastern section were the centre of the Median kingdom. Persia proper lay to the south in what is now the province of Fars, and Parthia proper was situated in the north-eastern section. The great cities of ancient times located within these boundaries were—Raghes, first and greatest; Arsacia, Ra and Ecbatana, and possibly Hecatompylos, the earliest capital of Parthia. The most important cities of the present time are—Tehran, the capital; Hamadan, commanding the site of the ancient Ecbatana; Casveen, distinguished once for its proximity to Almood, the capital and fortress of the Assassins; Rasht, the metropolis of the Caspian sea-coast; Kashan, once famous for the potteries in its vicinity, and now noted for its black scorpions; Koom, sacred for the shrine of Fatima, its burial-place of kings and queens; and Mashhad, "the holy," celebrated among Sheahs for the shrine of Imam Reza, the mausoleum of the great khalafah of Baghdad, and for its minarets and domes of gold. After these there is a number of second-rate cities and towns, such as Simnon, Savah, Sabzewar, Damgan, Sare and Barfrush, having each from five to ten thousand souls.

This entire region, desolate as it now is, was in time past the theatre of great events and is rich in antiquities.

Nothing is said in the Bible of the cities of this part of the country. Hamadan is the only place in it which has been identified with a Bible name. That city is believed to represent the Acmetha mentioned in the book of Ezra, and is thought to have been the burial-place of the famous Queen Esther and her kinsman Mordecai. The ruins of Ra are supposed to occupy the site of the Raghes mentioned in the apocryphal books of the Old Testament.

The people inhabiting the district I have described are for the most part of Persian stock, but there are many settlements of Turks and Kurds, and the Turkish blood is mingled with the Persian in the northern part of the country. The provinces of Gelan and Mazandaran are inhabited by what appear to be distinct races, differing from the people of other provinces. But all these races are Mohammedans except a few feeble and impoverished colonies of Jews, Armenians and Guebers. The last-named are so few as to form no factor of the population worthy of mention. The two first named are widely dispersed in small colonies in the cities and villages.

All the people, without exception of race or religion, are extremely poor, save a very few men who have inherited titles or been especially favored by the government. These men of wealth do not usually reside in the districts in which their estates lie, but resort to the capital and the large cities. The people live in villages composed of hovels constructed of sun-dried bricks or of mud. It is difficult to conceive of more forlorn and poverty-stricken abodes than are these huts of the poor peasants, nor can anything in the way of a village be imagined more forbidding than one of these clusters of huts compressed into the smallest space possible, so as to save expense and labor in building the wall with which the place must be enclosed. Especially dreary do these villages appear when they are constructed on a treeless plain and have no shade to relieve the sight of their brown and dingy walls. In many places, however, the unsightly walls are half concealed by the dense foliage of poplar, willow and sycamore trees, and the hovels are separated by gardens of many kinds of fruit trees, and the narrow streets resound with the ripple and fall of rills of crystal water.

The dress and appearance of the inhabitants of these villages are in keeping with the aspect of the hovels in which they live. The females are representatives of the domestic environments. As the traveler passes through the environs or the narrow streets he will see the women on the house-tops or in the streets. Many of them have the prescribed chadur, or outer mantle, in which custom requires them to appear, but it is often thrown loosely over the head and carelessly or not at all wrapped about the person. The faces of the women are in such places uncovered, and are seen to be careworn, sun-burned and begrimed with smoke and dirt. The garments are tattered and dirty, and nearly all the women have the look which tells of poverty, privation and the absence of the cheering and nobler incentives of life. The apparel of the men, as they are seen in their shops or fields, is not much better, but their faces and motions show the influence of the freer and more healthful life of the field, for they live much of their time in the open air. It could not be reasonably expected that such a people would be examples of cleanliness. In this particular they may compare well with the poor and degraded of other countries, but no European or North American country presents such a continuous, unmitigated pest of vermin as belongs to all places, persons and things in Persia. It is wellnigh impossible for the rich and the higher classes of the people to keep themselves free of the evil so long as they conform to the customs of the land. The peasants and masses of the people are covered with vermin. The servants of the rich are from these lower grades of society, and bear with them wherever they go the evidence of their contact with the people. The inns on all the roads are caravansaries and open to all travelers, and abused by all. The beggar and tramp may lie down to-night on the earthen floor in the room where to-morrow night the prime minister or the Shah may have to spread his carpet. A long train of camels and other beasts of burden bear the conveniences and luxuries of life required by a prince. His tent or his rooms, all that are available, are well furnished after the Oriental fashion, but the scores or hundreds of servants of the prince must shift for themselves, and find lodgings in the huts of the peasants and in the stables. From these places they come to the service of their royal masters. So accustomed are they to this manner of life that reform would be impossible unless their lords stood by them and gave to them daily the care required by infant children.

The places of public resort are free to all. In the mosques the people sit upon the floor; at home they spread their beds upon the floor. The public baths are underground dens reeking with filth. All the people feel the result of the defects of their civilization and habits of life. Some of the religious ablutions are beastly, and occasion habits which are prejudicial to the public health. Many of these habits are purely Oriental, and are practiced by non-Mohammedans. They are not entirely Mohammedan, though it should be known that the worst of them originated with the Mohammedan creed and are perpetuated by it. It may be said that Christian lands have hovels, paupers and filth. A Persian once said to me, "Show me in this land, if you can, any hovels more filthy than the huts to be seen in Ireland." But there is some relief from the curse in European countries. There are homes and inns and places of public resort where one may be safe from annoyance and the fear of it. But not so is it in Persia. In all the land the inns are no better than stables, and the keepers of them do not know what cleanliness is.

CHAPTER II.

Intellectual and Religious State of the People—Prominent Features of the Religious State—Persian Mohammedans extremely Religious—Excessive Attention to Externals—The Chief Element of Sheahism—The Divine Right of Ale—Sacredness of the Sayeds—Mohammedan and Protestant Devotions compared—Persian Superstition—Belief in Spirits and Demons: Deves, Jins, Ghouls—Departed Spirits—Faith in Talismans—The Evil Eye—Examples of Demoniacal Possession—Exorcists—Sacred Books possessing Supernatural Power—The Koran in Necromancy—The Armenian Bible—Other Books—Dreams, Faith in; Examples of—Superstition not Confined to the Lower Classes; Examples—Superstitious Ceremonies—Fears—Spirit of the Religious Orders—Characteristics—Learning Esteemed—Kind of Learning—Love of Religious Discussion—Sinister Motives in Discussion—Ascendency of the Secular Authorities over the Olema—Examples of the Methods of the Mullahs—Cases in Rasht and Ispahan—Controversial Books—Examples of Deception Universal—Deception as an Embellishment of Manners—Fraud the Great Barrier to Progress—Prevalent Vices: Intemperance; Opium-eating; Use of Tobacco; Adultery and Sodomy; Gambling.

MISSIONARY labor has to do chiefly with the moral and religious state of the people, but it is affected in some measure by every interest. It will be difficult for the reader of these pages to understand the needs of the Persians, the obstacles to be met by the missionary, or to perceive what has been accomplished, if he be ignorant of the intellectual and religious condition of these people at the beginning of missionary work. The religious creed leaves its trace in the mental state which it creates or cultivates.

If there were no restrictions to effort in behalf of Mohammedans imposed by the common law of the country, then missionaries would have to do chiefly with Mohammedans. But since the penalty of apostasy is supposed to be death, their labor is directed largely to Armenians and Jews. Yet much may be done directly and indirectly for the Mohammedan Persians. They are not, therefore, to be left out of a description of the people. Mohammedans constitute the bulk of the population, an overwhelming majority, in comparison with which the non-Mohammedans make but an insignificant company. Mohammedan influence is everywhere evident and paramount, and whatever affects them touches their subject races. For these and other reasons, which need not be stated here, the missionary is deeply concerned over their condition. I here note some of the prominent features of this condition.

They are extremely religious. Christianity does not in any place nor in any sect present such excessive concern for the externals of religion as does Sheahism. I believe that the Persians are more religious than Turks or Arabs. Their religious creed has all the essential doctrines of Islam and other tenets in addition. It has all the incentives of Suneeism to religious observances, and other motives which the Sunee has not. The chief doctrine of the Sheah sect is an element of enthusiasm additional to all that is furnished in the so-called orthodox faith. The doctrine of elective succession to the khalafate, the tenet of the Sunee, is less calculated to sanctify the object of choice than the doctrine of divine right, believed by the Sheah. He holds that the apostles of his order possessed by divine appointment their right to rule all Mohammedans. To him these persons are really objects of adoration. Immeasurable degrees of merit are obtained by the reverence of these apostles. In the course of time the number of sayeds has become too great for computation. Their tombs are conspicuous objects in nearly every village and city. To these shrines the people resort for the special benefits which are believed to be conferred by these saints.

A Sheah endeavors to observe all the ceremonies prescribed by the Koran and many others required by the traditions. He prays five times a day. Many ablutions are to be performed. A mistake in the repetition of the prescribed prayer makes a new effort at repetition necessary. One day in the week, if not oftener, he must go to the shrine of some sayed, and on Friday —his Sabbath—he must go to the mosque for public worship. Besides this, he has a penance in the form of an ablution or a prayer or alms to be performed as an atonement for certain sins. He must keep during the year many feasts, and must fast during the month of Ramazan. Sin, he believes, is obliterated and merit obtained by every repetition of the name of God and of a verse of the Koran or of a name of an Imam. It should not be supposed that a Mohammedan's prayer is so easy a thing as that to which a Protestant has been accustomed. His head must touch the earth in prayer. The Persian finds special merit in having his forehead touch a small cake of the sacred soil of Karbalah. With this cake of earth he is prepared to say his prayers in any place, and can safely kneel on his bed or on his carpet. But in every prayer he must consider well the points of the compass. All his devotions would be vitiated were he to bow his head toward any other place than the Kabah. There are movements and positions of the head, knees, hands and limbs which require great care and precision. The performances for the shrines are prescribed with minuteness. The Mohammedan is proud of his dexterity and grace of motion in prayer. In addition to the usual round of orthodox ceremonies, the Sheah has those which commemorate the Imams. These are the wailings of Moharam and of other seasons.

The Persian Sheahs are very superstitious. They have a great fear of the supernatural. This is a trait of the adherents of all false religions. The manifestations of this feeling are curious, and a refutation of the religion is often seen in the removal of the cause of superstition. The belief in spirits, demons and demoniacal possessions is common. There is much indistinctness in their notions of these superhuman beings. The names most commonly used to denote them are deves, jins and ghouls. The first named are devils, or evil beings supposed to inhabit forests and desert places, to exist in a human body of uncouth and fierce aspect and to possess superhuman power, but of satanic and evil intent. They are supposed to be influenced by Satan, the great deve. It is true, I believe, that the name is sometimes applied to wild animals, but only because of a fancied resemblance. The simple-minded peasants seem to think that the wild men, as apes and some other animals, are veritable deves. The jins are often confounded with the deves in the popular superstitions, yet a distinction is made between the two in the Koran. The former are commonly understood to be rational and invisible beings intermediate between angels and men, and are either good or bad. The Koran preserves something of the ancient myths concerning the genii, and furnishes the foundation for the notions entertained by the common people. The word *ghoul* is purely Persian, and is used to denote a being which is, in part, both man and beast, and which inhabits the desert. It is of great strength, but of little wisdom, and feasts on the bodies slain by the king of death. The conception seems to be essentially that of the old myth of the satyr modified by Persian imagination. The belief in the existence of these monsters is as commonly present as is the belief in the being of deves and jins: it furnishes the source of many of the large stock of Persian tales.

The belief in the return to earth of departed spirits is universal in Persia. So is the notion of the direct interposition in human affairs of both good and bad spirits. Evil spirits are thought to take possession of human beings because of sin or omission of a duty, as the neglect of a fast or a prayer. It might be conjectured that a mind filled with notions of this sort would be greatly disturbed by anticipation of danger. So it would be were it not for the fact that the power and influence of the evil beings may be broken by talismans, prayers, fasts and interpositions of saints. Bad spirits are supposed to cause harm to man or beast by what is called the "evil eye." The term is commonly used. It means that a person may look upon an object with such a sinful feeling as to cause an evil spirit to inflict some injury on the object. A person was looking at and admiring a beautiful donkey. When the owner mounted it and rode off the animal seemed to be lame. The owner could conjecture no other reason for the lameness except that the man who praised it had communicated to the creature the evil eye. Some persons are thought to have the power of summoning an evil spirit by a look of the eye. The power is an unfortunate possession, for most persons are anxious to be rid of a man having such a baneful influence. It is sometimes seriously charged by one man against another that he possesses this power and has used it for doing evil. The charge is sometimes made the pretext for extortion in the way of damages. A servant was once riding a fine horse down the mountain, when the animal fell and was seriously hurt. The only excuse made by the man to his master was that at the instant the horse fell he was admiring it and feeling great pride on account of the beauty and excellence of the horse, and must have given it an evil eye.

Another form of spirit interposition is in the way of demoniacal possession, by which is meant that an evil spirit enters a person, whom it controls continuously or periodically. Certain diseases are thought to come from satanic influence. Exorcism naturally follows belief in demons. There are professional exorcists. Some of the mullahs are believed to have power over spirits. Exorcists are not only known among Mohammedans, but with Jews and Armenians. Exorcism is a distinct function of an order of the clergy in the Armenian Church. To this office men are regularly ordained. The function is exercised by Armenians and Jews as a means of gain, and large sums are paid in some instances for casting out an evil spirit. The arts practiced for this purpose are many. The Koran or some other sacred book is read, prayers are recited and talismans used. The exorcist is often discreet enough to perceive that the supposed possession is the effect of disease, and he administers a nostrum which brings notoriety and the coveted reward. A man who had traveled over a wide extent of country using the pretended gift informed me that he had effected many cures. He seemed sincerely to believe the common superstition. It is not strange that one brought up among the people should so think. The exorcists of the Armenian Church are often put to it to find subjects on which to exercise their gifts. Their province, however, is understood to embrace, I believe, spiritual errors and corrupt agents, as well as the demons. The presence of this office in the Armenian Church may with reason be thought to have come from the earliest days of the Church.

The superstition of Persians invests all sacred books with supernatural influence. That power is shown in the control of spirits and in many other ways. A mullah, in discussing the merits of the Koran, related his own experience to me as evidence of the divine origin of that book. "One day," said he, "my knife was stolen. I did not know who had taken it, but I determined to try and find out the thief. I wrote a verse of the Koran on three strips of paper, and on the back of each strip I wrote the name of a suspected person. Then I made three little balls of clay, and put one strip of paper in each ball. I then put the balls in a basin of water. They all sank at once, but the clay of one soon parted and dissolved, and the paper which I had put in it rose to the top of the water. I read on it the name of the suspected person. I went to him and accused him of the theft. He immediately confessed, and gave up my knife. Such is the power of the Koran." The book is often suspended over the door or above the highway, that the charm of it may be felt by all who pass beneath it. It is laid on the sick. Its verses are written on bits of paper, and these are placed on those parts of the body which appear to be the seat of the disease. Some persons will not undertake a journey until a favorable omen has been obtained by opening the book at a passage understood to be prophetic of good luck. The stars are often consulted, but the Koran has to a great extent taken the place of the ancient astrology, though it should be said that the science of astrology is now closely connected with the mystic numbers and words of the Koran and other books.

The practice of seeking favorable omens is not confined to Mohammedans, but is common with Christians and other sects, each one using its own sacred books and paraphernalia of worship. The Armenian Bible is an oracle for Armenians in more ways than the true way. A like use of the Old Testament and of the Gammora is made by Jews. Sometimes an old Bible or other book is made famous for working miracles and effecting cures of disease, and the people come from far to receive the benefits of its charm.

Dreams are firmly believed to be revelations of future events. The knowledge of them has been reduced to a science. They have been carefully analyzed, and are divided into the portentous and the unportentous. The prophetic class are minutely described. But few of the people understand the complicated science. They are governed by their own forebodings as to the import of their dreams, and it is believed that they are not slow to invent dreams to meet exigencies of their callings. It is a common thing for a Persian to begin a request by relating a dream in which he describes in a very graphic way all the conditions which he hopes will be fulfilled by you. This belief is not confined to the illiterate, but is prevalent with all classes. A learned mullah, speaking to me of his faith in dreams and in the Koran, related the following: "Of all the members of the household, we honor and love the grandmother most. I loved my grandmother very much, and when she died I was lonely, and neglected to read the Koran as I used to do when she was living. After a time I forgot to read for the repose of her soul. So time went on: autumn came and the cool nights, and we took our beds from the roof and spread them at night in the court. But there came a change and the air was close and hot, so that I ordered that my bed should be taken to the roof again. One night I sat up in the court a long time after the other members of the family had gone to sleep, and I thought of many things which had happened in the past year. At last I went up to bed, having my cloak over me, and thinking I would lie down for a part of the night only, and that after midnight it might be too cold to remain on the roof. How long a time I had been there, and whether I was awake or asleep, I can hardly tell. I saw a form in indistinct outlines near the farther side of the roof slowly moving in the darkness. As I looked upon it, thinking it might be some member of my family, I saw that it came on toward me, and I could see something of the features. A chadur covered in part the head and shoulders and fell about the person. As the form came nearer in slow and measured motion and without seeming to touch the ground, I perceived that the eyes were intently fixed, that the face was serious and stern, and that an uplifted hand threatened me. As the spectre approached I discerned its unearthly look and bearing, and knew that a being from the unseen world was approaching. Springing from my bed as the spectre came nearer, and stepping backward, I cried, ' Who are you?' But the form silently continued its steady approach, coming frightfully near. I stepped backward; again it came on. I moved back again, looking all the time toward it. It came forward as I retreated, until at last I became conscious of a deeper darkness below me, and that I stood upon the verge of the roof, whence another step could not be taken. The thought flashed on my mind, 'This spirit intends to kill me.' Then, looking in despair and horror, I saw it was my grandmother. 'Oh, mother!' I cried, 'will you kill me? Spare me now, and I promise to offer the korbon and to read three suras on next Friday night.' I awoke. The next day I told my wife what I had dreamed, and I said,

'I have promised grandmother to read three suras on next Friday night. Do not let me forget it. If I do, she will kill me.' Friday night came. I had gone to bed, and was just about to put out the light when I thought of my promise. I arose and read the three suras. From that day to this, now nine years, my grandmother has not appeared to me. Such are the charm and power of the Koran."

These superstitions seem to be stronger with the higher classes and learned men than with the illiterate—a fact accounted for by the teachings of their religious books. A mujtaheed holding a high position, once conversing with me and speaking of the curing of the sick by prayers and charms, claimed to have cured many persons. When asked to describe the process by which he cured, he spoke of different things; among them was this—namely, to kindle a fire near the head and feet of the sick and to burn passages of the Koran written on bits of paper, also to burn prayers written for the purpose. It is impossible for a person who has not associated with Persians to understand the fear to which they are all their lives in bondage, or the heavy burdens in the way of religious ceremonies which they have put upon themselves. With them every act has its danger of defilement and its ceremony of purification. The tears shed in the religious weepings are bottled, and used to cure the sick and poured out as libations. Says one of the Persian teachers: "A tear shed in weeping

Mullahs.

for Hassan and Hosein will wash away the sins of a lifetime."

We can form no adequate conception of the amount of thought which must be given by these people to religious convictions. The superstitious mind is wonderfully prolific in the products of the imagination. These statements relate especially to Mohammedans, but they are true, to a great extent, of all the sects of Persia. The nominal Christians and the Jews feel the influence of their rulers, and there has been some rivalry between them and the Mohammedans in the matter of traditions and religious feasts, fasts and rites, and they have borrowed from one another. The cross, chalice, wafer, chrism and paraphernalia of the Church are invested by the imagination of Armenians and Mohammedans with a supernatural charm and virtue.

The spirit of the religious orders furnishes some insight to the religious state of the people. The mullahs may be called the priests of the Mohammedans. But Islam has no sacrificial service, and the mullahs are more properly termed teachers and preachers or ministers of religion. Many of them are ministers without a charge, and never officiate before a congregation. It is not my purpose to give here a description of the common offices and duties of these men: this has been written in another volume. I wish now to give an understanding of the spirit and temper of the mullahs, and to show how they are affected toward religious truth.

One notable feature of their condition is their great esteem for learning. They prize all learning, but especially that which they have been taught to consider such. The knowledge which they covet is that which they have been trained to consider most desirable: it is the knowledge of their own religious system. It may be true that many of these men are more desirous of the reputation for wisdom than for the actual possession of it, but even this desire shows that in their judgment learning has a value. It must be confessed that many of them are very zealous for knowledge, and very laborious in their pursuit of it. Some of them spend the greater part of a lifetime in preparatory study. We have in Christian lands but few examples of such long-continued and intense application of mind in the way of preparation as is furnished by the best representatives of Islam. It is a great pity that this zeal and labor are not directed to the investigation of all knowledge, or of something better than the theology and rites of Islam. In fact, the greater part of this study is devoted to the discussions on the proper manner of observing the rites—how these are vitiated and how made meritorious. As their whole system is one of justification by ceremonies, we can understand how important this study must be thought by them, and how valuable in their estimation a thorough knowledge of fasts, ablutions, prayers, pilgrimages and the whole round of rites must be. There is a course of secular study preparatory to the study of sacred things which they value for its relation to the latter. Arabic grammar, logic, astronomy and astrology are thought to be important subjects of study. These people have a very extensive literature relating to religious subjects. Many books have been written by Sheahs concerning the question of the succession in the khalafate and on the sayings and example of the twelve Imams. Persian mullahs have very little or no knowledge of geography, mathematics and the natural sciences. They know nothing of any branch of learning which could give them an acquaintance with anything outside of the range of their own religion.

Another prominent trait of these men is their love of discussion about religious matters. Some of them have gained from their own books and from controversial works some knowledge of the principal points of controversy between Islam and other religions, especially the Christian religion. They have the Koran's statements with reference to the divinity of Christ and the Trinity. Every book written against Mohammedanism is sure to call out one or more replies. They have, in Persian, works written in refutation of Judaism composed by apostate Jews, and in refutation of Christianity prepared by converts to Islam from the ranks of the nominal Christians. Controversy seems to possess remarkable power to stir up an evil spirit in these mullahs. Argument incites them to deeds of violence in a marked degree. They are wanting too much in honesty to feel the force of argument. This statement is true of the majority, not of all the ministers of Islam. It is commonly said by them that he who is not convinced by the proofs of Islam can be converted only by a club or a sword. Argument on their part is the commonly designed prelude to violence. The proofs of Islam, they say, are infallible, and it is the duty of all men to accept them: he who does not is worthy of death.

No confidence is to be reposed in the semblance of kindness and friendship with which the Persian begins his argument. His opponent is safe only when he has physical force at his command sufficient for his protection. Henry Martyn during his stay in Shiraz is said to have held many discussions with the Persian mullahs, but had there been no British government known to the olama of that city, Martyn would have fared badly, I conjecture. Tact and friendship may protect some persons and bring them great liberty of speech and action. These qualities sometimes protect the feeble from the rage of wild beasts. But I speak of Persians in general, not of exceptions. There has been great improvement within the past few years in the spirit and conduct of the olama. I will not speak of the reason of the change. But it is not so thorough and radical as to have abolished the disposition and custom of which I speak. The secular authorities have gained some advantage over the mullahs. The power of the priesthood is not so great in secular affairs as it once was. But it is yet common for mullahs to introduce a trial with argument to pave the way for violence. The usual expression with which a Mohammedan begins his argument is: "This discussion is to be continued until either you shall have converted me or I shall have convinced you." No words can truly describe the cruelty and violence to which Mohammedans resort when they have liberty to follow their inclinations. An Armenian was accused before a mujtaheed of Rasht of the crime of adultery. Obeying the summons, he came to the house of the mujtaheed and sat down on the pavement near the wall of the house while the mullah was hearing Mohammedan witnesses in an upper room. The instant that the mujtaheed pronounced the man guilty, one of his servants took an iron mangal full of live coals and threw it from the upper window upon the head of the condemned man as he sat in the court. The rabble then tied a rope to his feet and dragged the mangled body through the streets. It is true that the Shah reproved the conduct of the mujtaheed, but he inflicted no punishment except to consign the priest to a residence of several months in one of his palaces in the suburbs of Tehran. Several persons charged with being Baubs were arrested in a village about nine farasaks from Ispahan. The accused were brought before the shaik al Islam. The investigation opened with a discussion. One of the accused, Kazim, asked the shaik if he believed the New Testament, and on the shaik replying that he did, Kazim replied, "Then you must find testimony to Mohammed in the New Testament, for that book was written before Mohammed." Whereupon the shaik cried out, "Kafir! infidel!" and ordered that Kazim be slain. The man was then led away to the place of execution and beheaded.

I have mentioned the influence of controversial books in Persia. In illustration of this I will quote a few extracts from my journal: "After public worship to-day a rozakhan and two young mullahs remained to talk with us. After asking what proof I had that no other lawgiver or saviour should arise after Christ, and being advised to read the New Testament to find the answer of his question, the young man drew from beneath his coat a book written in Persian and entitled *Nusrat id Deen*, 'The Defence of the Faith,' and said that the book proved clearly the authority of Mohammed from both the Old and the New Testaments. The passages quoted from the Old Testament were such as declared the blessings of Esau, but no mention was made of the blessings of Isaac." Again: "I have been detained by a discussion with a mullah, who has been very inquisitive. He brought to me a book entitled *Sef ul Ommah*, 'The Sword of the People,' a controversial work of Islam. It was written by Hajah Mullah Ahmad. A Jewish rabbi of Kashan, near which city Ahmad lived, tells me that Ahmad sent his son to the Jewish rabbis to hear the Old Testament read and interpreted, with the express purpose of writing this book. He says also that the occasion inducing the mullah to write the work was the receipt by Fattah Ale Shah of a controversial work from London, to which the Shah desired that an answer should be composed. He says that Ahmad spent three years in the preparation of the book." Again I find this note: "There has been much discussion of late among the mullahs of Tehran. It appears that the book 'Scale of Truth' [*Mezon al Hak*] was reported to the mujtaheed Ah Said Saduk, who on reading it wrote a complaint to the governor of the city concerning the circulation and publication of such books. The governor replied that the work was published in India, and that he could not call the British government to account for it, but the best thing to be done was that he, Saduk, should compose an answer."

Love of controversy is not confined to Persian Mohammedans, but is a marked trait of all Persians. It has peculiar development with Sheahs. The Sheah enters into a controversy with a relish, and he is very certain to come out of it either a winner or mad as a hornet. But Persians of other beliefs show that they would do as he does if they could. If they have been instructed by him, they have been apt pupils.

Deception is another trait of Persian character. It should not be represented, as it has been by some travelers, as an amiable weakness and an excess of the good quality called courtesy. True, it enters into all the acts of a Persian's life. As an embellishment of manners it may be more tolerable than in other matters. But so strong is a Persian's propensity to put on the semblance of truth that every profession of his is to be received with allowance. The deception he practices is good evidence of his knowledge of the natural expression of truth. He can imitate or put on the outward appearance of every virtue and good quality. How can one dissemble so accurately without knowing what is truth? The semblance itself is proof of the perception of what is true and good. His deception as an embellishment of manners becomes in time intolerable, and as a means of paving the way to cruelty it is shocking. The verdant stranger and traveler in that land may be soothed with assurance given that after hours of weary riding he is now near the place of rest, and the assurance may give some spirit for the remaining long and tedious march; but when these delightful embellishments lead him into darkness where he expects light, and over rocks and a rugged way where he was led to believe he would find a smooth road, he learns that there is something more valuable than the ornaments of speech. The Persian may offer you his eye, his head, his house and his lands free, and to emphasize the generous offer may solemnly lay his hand on his heart or his eye; but the wayfarer may be assured that it is all for ornament, and that instead of giving, the cheat expects pay for everything, with an extra karan added for the courtesies and ornaments. The sober declaration made to me by a venerable mullah is very significant of the tendencies of Persians when he said, "During the blessed month of Ramazan all the people abstain from food and drink, and the better class abstain from lying also."

While these statements are true of the Persians as a whole, there are many Persians of intelligence whose word is reliable in the ordinary affairs of social and business life. But the insecurity of property and traffic through the prevalence of deception and fraud is, more than any other thing, the great barrier to commerce with Persia and to the general progress and improvement of that country.

Deception may be called a national vice in Persia, but it is not the only one. The prevalent vices in that country are nearly the same as are seen in other lands. The use of alcohol and intoxicating drinks is not a national vice of Persia. Mohammedan law and the public sentiment of the nation are against the manufacture, sale and use of all kinds of alcoholic and spirituous drinks. The proportion of drinkers to the Mussulman population must be very small. In the absence of statistics we are left to conjecture. Large quantities of wine and brandy are manufactured, and a large amount is imported. But the total amount is small compared with the products of the manufactories of other countries. There are no distilleries in the land. Whatever liquor is manufactured is made in the dwellings of Armenians, Jews and Guebers. In the cities there is a large number of drinkers, not only among non-Mohammedans, but among the Mussulmans also. Prohibitive orders are sometimes issued, but these are spasmodic efforts. The chief officers of state are sometimes the worst drinkers. The country at large, however, is wellnigh free from the sale and use of alcohol. There is not an open and public liquor-saloon in the kingdom. The manufacture and sale are the privilege and disgrace of the Christians and Jews.

Although such is the state of the liquor-traffic, the Persians make up for the loss of whiskey by the use of opium and tobacco. The proportion of opium-eaters and smokers may safely be conjectured to be as large as is the number of drinkers in other countries. There are many Persians who use the deadly hasheesh, and many take arsenic. No vice is so prevalent with Europeans as is the use of tobacco among Persians. Every Persian man and woman smokes the kalyon. This pipe is seen in every place where Persians are to be found. It is carried on the highway by every Persian traveler; it is seen in every shop in the bazar and in every dwelling in the land. The smoke of the kalyon is said to have a very injurious effect upon those persons who use it habitually. Although polygamy is permitted and there is no limit to the number of concubines allowed by the law of the land, yet Persians say that adultery and sodomy are both very prevalent. The license given in the way of marriage does not prevent the other vices. In fact, it may be believed that this license tends to the increase of the other two vices. The prevalence of sodomy is notorious. Although the nominal penalty of adultery is death by stoning, the severity of the punishment does not prevent the expectation of escape. The penalty is seldom inflicted. If the vice is as rare as the execution of the penalty, the kingdom might be thought to be a model of virtue. If sodomy be a common vice of the men, adultery is said to be a special vice of the women, by which they retaliate. The costumes of the females and the religious and social customs give favorable opportunities for amorous intrigues. The street-costume is so effectual a concealment of the person that no man is able to distinguish his own wife from other women in a public place, and custom forbids him to indulge his suspicions by any officious inquiry.

Gambling is common with Persians. Cards, chess and other games are used for this purpose, and the effects here are the same as those which are seen in other countries—namely, waste of time and loss of money, with drunkenness and other vices.

CHAPTER III.

Condition of the Women of Persia—Effect of Sheahism on the Popular Estimate of Women—Influence of Fatima—Effect shown by Persian Poetry—Popular Estimate of the Sayeds—Sanctity of Female Sayeds—A Woman's Power over her Husband—Chivalrous Spirit of Persians—Example of the Shah—Reverence of Persians for Maternity—Property Rights of Woman—Conditions Adverse to Woman—Lack of Schools for Females—Child-marriage—Female Seclusion—Woman's Costume—Effect and Prevalence of Polygamy—Baneful Effect of Sekah Marriage—The Non-Mohammedan Women of Persia: Jewesses, Christian Women—Contrasts—Influence of Islam—Degraded Condition of Christian Women—Efforts for the Redemption of Woman in Persia—Proportion of Male and Female Converts—Place Assigned to Women in the Churches—No Converts from Mohammedan Women.

THE condition of the native women of Persia is a subject worthy of consideration by itself. In the treatment of this topic we have to notice the difference in the social and moral status of Mohammedan and Christian women. The state of the former is determined, to a great extent, by the laws and customs of Islam, but not entirely by these, for these general principles are modified by the peculiar tenets of the sects. The Persians are Sheah Mohammedans, and the peculiarities of this sect have a marked influence over the estimate at which woman is held. This division of Islam owes its origin to a woman. The claim of the Imams to the supreme control of the Mohammedan world rests upon the right of succession in Fatima, the daughter of Mohammed and wife of Ale. This is not the only ground of the claim, but it is a valid one if the right to rule rests upon the right of inheritance. The Sheahs contend for the right of inheritance. The Sunees advocate the elective right in the congregation of believers at the first. The principle has long since been abandoned by them, and the sultan claims authority on the ground of heredity. Fatima, having the right of succession, is necessarily a person greatly revered by Sheahs. The ruling sect of the Sheahs is that called the "Twelve," and is strongest in Persia. The chief tenet is that the right of the khalafate belonged to the direct descendants of Fatima and Ale to the twelfth generation, the succession ending in the Mahde. The place which Fatima fills in Persian history and tradition has a marked influence over the sentiments of Persians toward woman. The place given to her must raise the popular estimate of woman in general. That such has been the result is shown by the poetry and much of the literature of Persia, as also by the religious ceremonies and the common life of the people. Persia is the only country of the Mohammedan world in which poetry has been to any great extent cultivated. It was not until the Sheah faith asserted its power that Persian poetry began to flourish. The poetical element may be naturally more marked in Persians than in other Mohammedans, but it seems to be true that Sheahism has cultivated that element. Much of the poetry is in praise of Fatima, and, unconsciously to Persians, inspires noble sentiments toward her sex.

Fatima is the mother of the sayeds. The female members of this sacred class are held in no less reverence than the male descendants of the first Sheah. The sayeds are the direct descendants of Fatima and Ale. They now compose a countless multitude, and are commonly distinguished from other Mohammedans by the green turban. They are often found in large communities and intermarry. In many places they hold lands under grants from the crown. Although the lineage is reckoned in the male, yet it is thought to be more honorable when both parents are of the house of Fatima. To wed a sayed is thought to be a great honor, and she is not slow to assert the rights of her order and family. Even though she may be married to a man of common blood or a peasant, her relation to the founder of the national faith commands respect and makes her a distinguished person in her own circle of friends. She will resent a wrong done to her as a crime committed against the whole line of saints. An appeal by her to her neighbors is sure to bring down the wrath of the community in which she lives upon the offender, and every one has a superstitious fear of her person and character.

Shah of Persia. Page 61.

Woman gains some advantage in Persia from the chivalrous spirit of Persians. It is thought to be unmanly for a man to resent the ire of a woman. If she meets him in a public place, she may take off a shoe from her foot and slap him in the face with it, but he dare not retaliate by beating her. He will show his sense of honor by standing patiently while she punishes him, rather than incur the disgrace of having lifted a hand against her or having fled from her. There is hardly any disgrace which a Persian dreads more than to be assailed by a woman in a public place. It is related that the Shah was once riding in the street when at a certain point on the way he was met by a company of women who implored protection from the extortion of his vazier. This man had, in collusion with the bakers, raised the price of wheat and bread. The Shah escaped as best he could from the crowd, and turned into one of his gardens. Seating himself on the porch of his summer-house, he ordered the vazier to be brought to him with a rope about his neck. When the man came near the Shah said, "Why have you put me to shame? Why have you raised the price of wheat?"—"For your sake," replied the vazier. "The wheat is in your granary, and the purchase was made for your benefit."—"Yes," replied the king, "but you have dishonored me by bringing all the women out against me.—Strangle him!" cried the Shah. But now the king's favorite appears and intercedes, and the man's life is spared. It should not be thought that the Persians are so amiable that they always act with this forbearance. In his own home the man is not tardy in asserting his authority, and custom gives him the right to whip his wife as well as his children. In many cases, however, it is dangerous for him to exercise this prerogative. I have heard Persians say that it is important in selecting a wife to take one who will bear the rod with docility.

Reverence for maternity has its influence in protecting woman in Persia. This feeling is inculcated by the Koran. The sentiment, very strangely as it would seem, centres in the grandmother. She is the most honored member of the family. The children respect her more than they do their own mother. She is to them the model of motherhood. The practice of polygamy seems to give special occasion for the exercise of the maternal feeling in the parent and the filial sentiment in the son. The lack of the husband's affection is supplied by the love of the child. The son regards his mother as an object of his protection. She looks to him for solace and support. She is his chief mourner at his decease, but should he survive her his is the most heartfelt sorrow.

A Persian woman is protected by the law in the possession and sole use of all property inherited by her. Her husband has no right to the property. But this right of hers is not always protected, although the law is clear. Her title, however, is usually maintained. There is no effort made in Persia by Persians for the education of women and girls. Many of the Mohammedan women are readers. Whatever learning they acquire is obtained from private tutors. It is rarely the case that a woman learns to do more than read; the majority of females cannot do that. The colleges in the mosques are for male students; there is no provision for woman's education. The custom of child-marriage is against her. The Mohammedan girl is of age at nine. She usually marries before her thirteenth year, and goes to the control of her mother-in-law, and has the charge of a family and the work of a household. If she is of the peasant class and poor, she will labor in the field besides attending to her domestic duties. Yet women do not commonly perform the work of men in the field.

The custom—or rather theory—of Persians requires woman's seclusion. Her costume is a sign of this seclusion, and the greater and more inconvenient part of it. With peasants and the poor there is practically no harem, and little or no appearance of retirement except the wearing of the chadur, the loose cotton cloth or mantle which is thrown over the head, and which may be instantly wrapped about the person if it be desired to conceal the face from a stranger. On all ordinary occasions the chadur is laid aside while the woman is at work. It is only the very rich who can carry out into every-day life the Eastern theory of the harem.

The system of polygamy is the great cause of the Mohammedan woman's degradation and misery. It is true that the practice is impracticable to a great many. Many Persians have but one wife. But the influence of the law and the public sentiment created by the system have all the effect upon her condition of the universal practice of the custom. The system takes from her all confidence in the permanency of the affection of her husband. It prevents all expectation of permanence in the marriage relation, because she agrees in the marriage contract to a divorce at the will of her husband. It fosters feelings of jealousy and occasions intrigue in the household. It should not be thought that poverty is any barrier to the practice of polygamy; the rich men do not commonly have the largest number of wives. The men who are least able to bear the expense are often found to have several wives.

Of all the social and religious customs, no one is more baneful in its influence over women than the custom of Sekah marriage. This is a system of concubinage under which there is no limit to the number of wives, and no requirement respecting the continuance of the relation except the agreement made by the contracting parties. It is legalized prostitution sanctified by a brief religious rite. However bad the physical effects of this system may be, these are not the greatest of the evils resulting from it. The effect on the woman's sense of honor and self-respect and on the morals of the people is yet more fatal. When marriage is treated by the law and religion as so light and trifling a matter, the people very naturally come to think that it is of no great sanctity, but a matter of convenience only.

These statements relate to the Mohammedan women especially, and not to all the non-Mohammedans. There is no very marked difference between the state of the Jewish and Mohammedan women. There is some pride of race and of religion which protects, in some degree, the Jewess; but the customs and laws of Islam are drawn very largely from the Old Testament. In the marriage contract the right of divorce by the husband is acknowledged by the woman and is at the man's option. Sekah marriages are frequent among Jews, but not so common as with Mohammedans. Polygamy is lawful and is practiced among the Jews. Jewesses are excluded from the synagogues and from the schools. They are assigned to the gallery without, and obtain their view of what is passing in the synagogue through small holes left in the walls. By this arrangement there is a painful and sham attempt to perpetuate the distinctions made in the appointments of the tabernacle and temple by the separate courts for the men and for the women. No arrangement of a Persian synagogue is more effective to show woman's degradation and the vile, heartless character of the men than this outer gallery arranged for the females.

Of all the women of Persia, the Christian women, even in the unreformed state of the Oriental churches, occupy the most honored place and have the happiest lot. But their condition is degraded by the influence of Mohammedan laws and customs. That influence requires conformity to Mohammedan notions of dress and seclusion—not in all particulars, but in many respects. It also inculcates in men ideas of women which are contrary to Christian precept and influence. Armenian women wear the street-costume of Mohammedan females whenever they go upon the street. At home a handkerchief is worn over the mouth, tied about the lower part of the face and around the neck. Whatever other purpose it may serve, this indicates silence and submission, and is often thought to be a very important and useful custom, as any one would judge it to be who has heard the epithets and the torrent of words which a Persian woman can use when once she opens her mouth. An Armenian woman once poured out a flood of impudent words upon a man who had reproved her, when the man answered by a slap on her mouth. The woman complained to the priest, but he replied that had she kept the handerchief over her mouth she would not have suffered the indignity.

Notwithstanding the Mohammedan environments, the Armenian women have an evident superiority in personal comeliness, truth, chastity and all moral qualities, while in domestic happiness, security in the love of husband and family, permanency of the marriage relation, safety of life, possessions and honor, the comparison is all to their advantage. Whatever is hard in their lot is due mainly to the corruption of their own Christian

Armenian Women.

doctrine and practice and the power of a Mohammedan government. They are lacking, however, in intelligence, knowledge and purity and in the whole current of life. It is rarely the case that any Armenian women of the rural districts can read or write. In one suburban Armenian village, in a population of some two hundred souls, not one woman could read the Armenian Scriptures. Armenians of the cities offer a more favorable estimate.

The question arises in this connection, "What has been or can be done to improve the condition of the women of Persia?" Nothing has been done except the expedients adopted by missionaries. There has been no marked change in Mohammedan laws and social customs. The missionaries have done something in the way of mission-schools. Not more than two hundred, however, of all the million females receive the direct benefit of this education. The influence exerted in behalf of woman by female missionaries should not be despised. In time it will affect large numbers of the people, but it cannot be expected to do all that should be done for a radical change of woman's status in Persia. The growth of Protestant Christianity will be in her favor, but Protestantism must suffer the power of Oriental social laws so long a time as Mohammedanism remains. Woman never can attain to much excellence under these laws. Her future is determined by the same conditions which fix the fate of all the people of Eastern lands. Much may be done by individual conversions, the education of some and the improvement of a few communities; by this means an efficient contribution may be made to the general and public good. But a radical and general improvement of the people can come only with the complete overthrow of the Mohammedan political power.

There is a marked contrast in the proportion of male to female converts in Eastern Persia and in America and other Christian lands. In the latter there is a decided excess of females. In Persia the opposite is true. The number of accessions to the churches from the male population exceeds the number of additions from the female. There are two marked reasons for this difference. The men are by custom the leaders in all public assemblies and changes. Mohammedan women attend the mosques, Armenian women attend the churches, but not in such numbers as do the men. When they go to these places of public resort they must be closely veiled and must occupy a retired part of the auditorium. Another reason for the difference is the stronger prejudice and superstition of the women. They hold to the old religion more firmly than their fathers and brothers do. Reason and argument have less weight with them to convince; but, on the other hand, their opposition is less decided and active. The place assigned to the native woman in the old churches is either a gallery or the rear of the auditorium, where a railing or picket separates her from the place given to the man. In the mosques the women occupy one side of the room, as in some parts of Europe and America the division is made between the sexes. In mosques all the congregation sit or stand facing the Kabah, or place of prayer. In the tazeahs, or religious theatres, the men and women occupy separate sides of the room, sitting face to face, the women being veiled. I am not aware that any Mohammedan woman of Persia has become a Christian, although several Mussulmans have made a profession of their faith, and many have shown their dissatisfaction with Islam.

CHAPTER IV.

Particular Account of the Opening of the Mission in Eastern Persia—Appointment of Mr. Bassett to Tehran—Tour of Exploration—Departure of Mr. Bassett and Family from Oroomiah for Tehran—Snowstorm—Incident in a Balakhanah of Kilishkin—Last Stage of the Journey—Mrs. Bassett.

HAVING introduced my readers to the country and people of Eastern Persia, so that they will understand some of the principal environments of the missionaries and mission-work in that country, I will now give a more particular account of the mission in the part of the country I have described.

The occupation of Eastern Persia by resident American missionaries began with the settlement in Tehran of Rev. James Bassett in the fall of 1872. We speak of this settlement as the occupation of Eastern Persia, because the charge of work in Hamadan and also the supervision of native itinerant work in Khorasan was specially given to Mr. Bassett. At this time there was no mission of any Protestant society in the capital, nor had any been established in that city at any previous time. Excepting the independent work carried on in Ispahan by the British missionary Rev. Robert Bruce, the American mission in Oroomiah was the only Protestant mission in the kingdom of Persia at that date. The mission in Oroomiah was founded in 1834 expressly for labors among the Nestorian Christians of Western Persia. But in 1871 this mission was transferred from the American Board in Boston, now the Missionary Board of the Congregational churches of the United States, to the Presbyterian Board of Foreign Missions, having its office in the city of New York, and plans were formed for the enlargement of the work of the mission so as to embrace the chief cities of Persia; and the mission was henceforth known by the name of the "Mission to Persia." In pursuance of these plans Mr. Bassett was appointed, while the mission was yet practically confined to Oroomiah, to occupy Tehran or Hamadan as he might think most expedient on visiting these two cities. The extended tours made by this missionary in the spring and summer of 1872 were preparatory to the occupation of one of these cities by him. He traveled from Oroomiah to Tehran *viâ* Tabriz. From the capital he journeyed to Hamadan and Senah, returning to Oroomiah on the 18th of July. He remained in that city until the 2d of November, expecting during the last ten days of this time to be joined by a missionary from the United States, who would go on with him to Tehran, where it seemed most expedient to begin work at that time. The lady missionary appointed in America to go to the capital is said to have been unable, owing to ill health, to proceed farther than to Constantinople, from which place she returned to the United States. The gentleman referred to preferred to remain in Oroomiah. Mr. Bassett, therefore, with his family, consisting of his wife and three children, left Oroomiah, as stated, for Tehran, going by way of Tabriz. The party reached the capital on the 29th of November. They were favored with fair weather and dry roads until they came into the vicinity of Casveen. Hastening on because of the lateness of the season and to save the extra distance of the circuitous route of the plain, they crossed the spur of the Elburz between Horumdarah and Kilishkin, and on the summit of the pass encountered the first snowstorm of the season. They suffered no special inconvenience from the cold, for they had taken all needed precautions against it, and the distance over the pass was but one day's journey. Mrs. Bassett rode with one of the children in a taktravan; the other two children had their large covered and padded baskets in which they rode, the two baskets being swung, pannier style, over the back of a horse. The taktravan was well lined with felt to exclude the cold.

At Kilishkin the party occupied a balakhanah, or chamber of the inn, the lower rooms being unfit to use. The chamber was constructed, Persian fashion, with five doors on one side of the room and opening over the court, and intended to be open in the summer. But it was now cold and stormy weather, and they were closed, though some of the fastenings were loose. While the other members of the party were busy here and there, the baby crept to one of the doors, and, raising herself to her feet by the aid of the door-frame, she put her hands and weight on the door, when it instantly flew open and the child fell out and over the doorsill; but her father happened to be near, and saw her just in time to put his foot upon the few inches of the long skirt yet passing over the sill: this prevented the fall. The child was suspended between the door and the stone pavement below by the end of her long skirt, and so saved from a fall from the chamber upon the stones.

The highlands, where cold weather might be expected, having been passed, the party came upon the lower country of the plains of Casveen and Tehran, and traveled more leisurely and without sickness or harm. The last stage of the journey was made from near Meanjub and along the upper road to the village of Kend. From this road they had in the entire distance a view of the plain of Tehran on their right, and from near Kend for the first time they saw the capital. With what interest did they look upon this city now spread out before them, not only because of its relation to themselves as their prospective home and the end of a long and tedious journey, but also because of its relation to the future of mission-work in Persia!

They entered the city by the gate called "Asp Davon," or horse-race—so named from the fact that the road leading to the race-course passes through it—and proceeded to the house prepared for their reception in the northern quarter of the city, known as Shimron gate. It is a fact of interest that Mrs. Bassett was the first American lady to enter the capital of Persia. If we take into the account her journey of the previous year from Trebizond, she had within the last fourteen months traveled in a taktravan and by caravan, and with an infant in arms, not less than a thousand miles. Yet she wrote at the time that she had never been in better health nor more happy than when thus journeying in the heart of Asia.

CHAPTER V.

Tehran, Situation of—Temperature and Climate—Antiquity of Tehran—Changes in—Later Improvements—Population: Armenians, Jews, Guebers, Mohammedans—Mullahs and Shah—Foreign Legations—State of Society—Mission-Work previous to 1872—Prospective Work of the Missionary—Native Assistants—Religious Toleration—School Opened—Armenian Elders—Baron Matteos—Proposed Union of Schools—Departure of the Shah for Europe—Prime Minister—Shah's Wife—Conspiracy—Erection of a Chapel—Congregation at the Chapel—Opposition of the Archbishop and Elders—Action of the Authorities—Schemes Defeated—Armenians of Feruzbahrom and Zard Aub—Summer Retreat—Vanak—Violence of the Priests—Intemperance of the Villagers—Priest Megerditch—Heat of the Country—Sickness—Increase in Schools—Annual Meeting in Oroomiah—Return to Tehran—Rains and Floods—Persian Houses—The Work in Hamadan—Mechail and Reforms—Priest Oracale—Persecution—Transfer of Native Preachers.

AS we now enter a new field of missions destined to play an important part in the evangelization of the land, some account of the city which is the chief centre of the field seems to be pertinent to the subject and may be of interest to the reader.

Tehran, the present capital of Persia, is situated on the northern side of a broad plain which runs nearly due east and west at the base of the Elburz Mountains, and opens into the north-western corner of the desert of

Khorasan. From the city there is an unbroken view to the south-east far into the desert. But between the capital and the barren regions of the desert proper there intervene the fertile plains of Ra and Varomene, stretching, together, a distance of some forty miles. The city stands within a semicircle of the Elburz and on the lower slope and southern face of Mount Shimron, one of the highest peaks of this notable range. To the north-east, some forty miles, the summit of the cone of Damavand rises to the height of twenty thousand feet above the level of the sea. The top of Shimron gains an altitude of nearly thirteen thousand* feet above the sea and nine thousand two hundred and fifty feet above the plain of Tehran. The environments, in the way of mountain and plain, are on a broad and grand scale, but they carry with them no cheerful and refreshing prospect, and can please, if at all, only by the feeling of grandeur which they inspire.

This plain, although it is nearly two hundred miles in length, has no considerable stream of water in it. The Karaj, a small river, rises northward of Tehran, and, breaking through a rocky barrier in a narrow gorge, enters the plain some twenty-five miles westward of the capital. It flows southward across the plain and along the southern side of it, and at no point in its course is nearer the city than fifteen miles. The city, therefore, has no source for the supply of water except the con-

* 12,750 feet.

Tehran from the Ispahan Road.

naughts which have been excavated along the lower slope of Shimron. Near the foot of that mountain there is the appearance of some fertility, and the plain is dotted with villages, but in the greater part of it naught is seen but a treeless and arid waste, on which a glaring sunlight shines from a cloudless sky, and over which hot winds from the desert blow during half the year. The Elburz serve as a barrier to the winds from the Caspian Sea and the north. Clouds gather about the lofty cone of Damavand, but vanish as soon as they approach the heated borders of the plain. In the winter the mountains and plain are covered with snow and swept by strong winds. The former become impassable. The plain is not long covered with snow, great as the altitude is. The greatest degree of cold on the plain of Tehran is rarely below 10° Fahrenheit. The climate is distinguished for equability. The changes of the seasons come on very gradually. The healthfulness of this region varies greatly in short distances, owing no doubt to differences in the irrigation and drainage of the lands. In former years Tehran was afflicted with malarial and typhoid fevers, but of late there has been great improvement in the sanitary condition of the city, and it will now compare favorably with the most healthful places in the kingdom. It is the custom, however, of the European residents and of many of the natives to resort to the mountains in the hot season. Some four miles northward of the capital there is an extensive cluster of villages known as Shimronaut. These villages are the principal summer resorts. The whole district is dotted with the white tents of the army and of refugees from the heat and the mosquitoes and gnats of the plain.

The importance of Tehran dates from the occupancy of the place, then a small village, by Agah Mohammad, the first of the Kajar tribe to obtain control of the kingdom and the founder of the Kajar dynasty. He was crowned king of Persia in 1796, but he made Tehran a rendezvous for his forces as early as 1776. After the erection of palaces and government buildings there was a gradual growth of the city until the year 1867, when the place is supposed to have had about sixty thousand inhabitants. At this date improvements were begun, and were carried on in the following years. The old walls were torn down, the area enlarged and a new moat dug. The newly-added area was laid out in wide streets after the plan of European towns. The improvements of a few years have made a very great change in the aspect of the city, rendering it more tolerable as a place of residence. It is now much more populous than when these changes began to be made. The tendency of the population in Oriental countries is to the capital. It is significant that the growth of Tehran has been greater in the last fifteen years than in the whole period of its previous existence, an interval of ninety-seven years. The growth is owing chiefly to the improved policy of the government. The reign of Nasir id Deen Shah has been one of peace. He has encouraged intercourse with foreign governments; he has made special effort to improve the capital. The increasing attractiveness of the capital has been felt by the people of other cities, to the loss of the latter. Comparatively little improvement has been made in other towns, but Tehran has grown with a rapidity equal to that of the most prosperous cities of other countries. The growth compares favorably with that of some of the flush towns of the United States. It is barely a decade older than the city of Cincinnati, and has nearly as large a population. This, considering the entire period of its growth, is certainly remarkable, especially for an Oriental city. The actual rapidity of progress is much greater than this statement indicates, for the larger part of the increase has been in the last fifteen years.

The population of Tehran is representative of all the races in Persia. The Persian and Turkish stocks predominate. The Persian language is the language of law and literature. On the opening of the mission the number of Armenians in Tehran was about one hundred and ten families. Seventy households were located in five suburban villages. The Jews claimed three hundred houses. The Guebers were not more than one hundred and fifty souls. The number of Europeans was estimated to be one hundred, of whom one-half were English-speaking people. The balance of the population was Mohammedan. The Armenians were settled in two quarters of the city—one on the south-eastern side of the town, near the old gate called Shah Abd al Azeem; the other on the western side, near the Casveen gate. The former community was the earlier settlement and numbered forty households. The latter had seventy households, and was made up by removals from the first colony. In each section there was an Armenian church and an officiating priest. The churches were dark and dismal places, built in the old style. They were constructed of sun-dried bricks. A railing or picket fence in the rear of the audience-room separated the women's apartment in the church from that of the men and from the altar. The priests read the service in the ancient Armenian language, a speech unknown to the worshipers. A school had recently been opened in the western settlement, and a teacher had been imported from Constantinople. He was a member of the Roman Catholic Church, but did not profess to be in the employ of the Romanists. There was no free tuition, and the children of the poor were excluded.

The Armenians, with few exceptions, are poor and ignorant; especially so are the inhabitants of the villages. Among the Armenians of the city were several Russian subjects, much superior to their Persian co-religionists in intelligence and wealth. These men were leaders in the Armenian community, and some of the Persian Armenians were of high rank and in the employ of the Persian government. By virtue of their descent

Jews of Tehran. Page 87.

from Georgian princes they received pensions from the Shah.

The Jews of the capital trace the origin of their colony to the settlement of Hebrews in the village of Damavand, which is near the mountain of that name. The place is about thirty miles eastward of Tehran. There was a colony settled here a long time before the founding of the Kajar capital. Some thirty families and the graves of their ancestors are the only memorials of the early colony. The Jews in Tehran are located in the eastern part of the city. The place is distinguished for poverty and filth. The people appear to have been more prosperous in former times than now. They gathered here from many places in the kingdom. Only those who had some property could live in the capital, but here the steady weight of Moslem rule has tended to their impoverishment and ruin. They possess ten synagogues, but every one of these, with a single exception, is no more than a small room in a dwelling-house. Jewesses are not permitted to enter these rooms, but are consigned to an outer gallery or vestibule, where they must see and hear through little holes left in the brick walls. In three of the synagogues schools were taught, but the course of instruction consisted of teaching the pupils to read the Hebrew Scriptures and traditions and to write the rabbinical character. The most influential men of the colony were physicians. Some of the Jews have been honored by the Shah and have good places, but the greater portion of them follow disreputable pursuits. They, as the Armenians and Guebers also, are manufacturers of wine and alcohol. They are fortune-tellers and exorcists, and they furnish secret retreats where Mohammedans can drink with impunity. The rabbi must slay every animal which is eaten, and the blood must be shed while he repeats a formula. The Feast of Tabernacles is celebrated in booths erected in the courts of the houses, for the people fear to make these on the house-tops, lest they should be seen by their Mohammedan neighbors and they should suffer violence. On Saturdays and other sacred seasons the long veil is worn during the service of the synagogue.

The Guebers of Tehran are, for the most part, merchants from Yezd. They deal in cotton, silk and woolen goods manufactured in Yezd and Kerman. Their religious rites are practiced in secret, if at all. They have erected a "tower of silence" for the exposure of the dead on the side of a desolate mountain about six miles south-eastward of Tehran and overlooking part of the ruins and plain of Ra. The top of the tower is arranged with niches for the reception of the dead bodies. It is intended that the vultures shall consume the flesh, but these birds seem to be easily satiated: that which they leave is burned and the ashes and the unburned remains are thrown into a pit in the centre of the structure.

The most noteworthy institution of the Guebers at

Burial-Tower and Plains of Ra and Tehran.   Page 91.

this time was a seminary for the education of the youths of both sexes. The school was under the management of an agent of the Parsees from Bombay. He resided in Tehran for the purpose of protecting the interests of his people in Persia. He brought funds from India, but these were so unfortunately invested as to occasion much loss and in great part to compel the abandonment of the educational scheme. The leaders of this movement represented the advanced class of the Parsees of India. Their school was ordered after the English schools, so far as ability permitted it to be. The studies were those of the English course. The religious doctrines and ceremonies of the Guebers were not conspicuous features of the instruction and discipline. The mission was of great service to the Guebers in many ways. By intercession with the Persian authorities the taxes were reduced or remitted wholly, and the Guebers enjoyed more liberty and security than before the establishment of the mission of the Parsees. There was some prospect of enlightenment for these people, if not of religious reformation, and the lack of the largest success in the movement seems to be an occasion of regret to all the friends of progress.

With reference to the Mohammedan population of Tehran very little need be added to that which has been previously written. It will be remembered that the Persian Mohammedans are of the sect called the "Twelve;" but the fact that they are considered by the

Turks or Sunees to be heretics does not appear to affect their feelings toward other religions. It has been assumed that they are more tolerant than Sunees because they have themselves been called heretics and have been persecuted. It is possible that there may be some difference in the feelings of these two great Mohammedan sects toward Christians. The difference, we think, is hardly perceptible, and if there really be any it is to be attributed more to natural temper than to religious faith, and is due rather to political relations than to either of the other motives. The mullahs of the capital exert some influence over their order in the rural districts. It is not, however, the priesthood, but the secular government, which determines the measure of religious toleration. The religious orders may intimidate the people and greatly influence the Shah and his court. The Shah is a sincere and, possibly, a superstitious Mohammedan, but either his policy or his natural disposition has led him to exercise a measure of liberality which could hardly be looked for in one of his creed.

In 1872 the foreign governments represented at the court of the Shah were—England, Russia, France and Turkey. In the course of the next thirteen years there were also the legations of Austria, the United States of America and Germany. The American missionaries were under the protection of the British legation; that is, so far as the mission had any representations to make to the Persian authorities, such were made by the British

Guebers' Burial-tower.

Page 95.

legation. These representatives were provided with commodious buildings in the city and on Shimron. This year the British minister occupied, for the first time, the new premises in the northern part of the city. The buildings had recently been constructed. The old legation was in the southern quarter, and had been sold to a Persian. The gentlemen connected with the legations and the chiefs of the telegraph corps were men of cultivated minds and manners. But it is to be said of many of the foreigners that their morals were not as good as their manners, and were not such as their social and official standing might lead one to expect. By contact with foreigners many of the natives were demoralized. Armenians especially felt the influence of the association, and female chastity was put at a low estimate by native women and foreign residents, while as yet the presence and influence of English and American women were unknown. The utter lack of a moral sense in the natives when their virtue is tried by the prospect of gain is conspicuous and deplorable. In the case of Mohammedans this lack is supplied by a severe law with a terrible penalty which guards the sanctity of the Mohammedan home, but no such law has been enacted for Armenian households or for the non-Mohammedan people: they are left to the exercise of their own religious laws and liberty. It is true that the greatest licentiousness prevails among Mohammedans, but under conditions which protect the Mohammedan home from pollution by foreigners. The Christian law may be plain enough, but that is set aside by the unscrupulous. Armenian parents sold their daughters to foreigners to live in wedlock for a limited period. The practice was followed openly and without shame. In this way Armenian women became mistresses of foreign legations, and were conspicuous for an extravagant and luxurious style of living. Such relationship to foreigners was supposed to be a source of wealth and was greatly coveted by Armenian females. But in the course of a few years there has been a marked change in this particular, attributable to the influence of American and English families and Christian agencies.

The Roman Catholic mission had been established in Tehran for some years, but its growth up to this time was small indeed compared with its expansion in the period covered by this narrative. Competition with Protestants appears to have been an important factor in the late enlargement of this mission. At this time there was no Protestant mission in the capital, and none had ever been established here. A Nestorian colporteur was sent from Oroomiah to this city in 1870. He opened a bookstall in the bazar, and frequently preached in private houses, especially in the house of Mr. Tyler, an English gentleman and a teacher in the Shah's college. He was here during the severity of the famine, and left for India in 1872, and thence returned to his home in Oroomiah.

To the missionary in Tehran was committed the

founding of the church and the opening of mission-work there, and the supervision of the work previously begun in Hamadan. He and his family were now separated from all missionary associates by the distance from Tehran to Oroomiah, not less than five hundred miles. The nearest mission of any society was that of Mr. Bruce in Ispahan. There was no mission-station on the east between Tehran and India. At this time it was impossible to obtain any suitable Nestorian preacher to aid in the work in the capital. Mechail, an Armenian of Hamadan, had been called to meet Mr. Bassett in Tehran to aid in secular matters. A Nestorian named Baba accompanied the missionary from Oroomiah as a colporteur. He rendered efficient help as a lay worker in the villages and bazars. During the winter the missionary resided in the northern part of the city. He applied himself to the study of the Persian language, and preached in the Turkish to Armenians who assembled at his house. In the following year he preached in the Persian tongue.

In the beginning of the mission in Tehran it was to be remembered that religious liberty had not been given by the Persian government to its Mohammedan subjects. The law of the land, as commonly understood, does not permit a Mohammedan or the child of a Mohammedan to change his religious faith, and the penalty for apostasy is death. It is true that the law is, commonly, no more nor less than the caprice of the ruler, and that caprice is fertile in expedients for doing whatever the ruler desires to do. But the religious authorities have great power, and the secular authorities may yield to the priests, and the caprice of the ruler may accord with their decisions. It was not certain that the government would permit missionaries to use the Persian language in Christian worship and instruction. It was also a serious question whether the secular authorities would permit the circulation of Christian books in that language. In view of the intolerance of Islam, as well as from considerations of special gain to the mission cause, all previous missions in Persia, except that of Mr. Merrick, had been designed expressly for some non-Mohammedan sect, as the Nestorians, Armenians, Jews or Guebers, and the religious or race language of the sect has been taken by the missionary as his specialty and as a medium for instructing the people of the sect for whom he labored. In Tehran the number of Armenians was so small as to make the sphere of mission-work very contracted if effort were to be confined to them. If the missionary were to labor for them exclusively, and the Armenian language were acquired for this purpose, Jews and other people could not be reached. But all the people know the Persian. It was decided, therefore, to carry on the work in the Persian language so far as the labors of the missionary were concerned, in the hope that the religious instruction would be available to every sect and race. The decision has been justified by results, and the plan adopted has been continued during the subsequent years. Whatever may be said with reference to the methods of work in other fields, this is undoubtedly the one best adapted to the condition of the people in Tehran.

Early in the spring (March 6, 1873), at the request of several Armenians, a school was opened near the Casveen gate. An Armenian named Lazar was employed to teach: he was not then a converted man, but subsequently he gave evidence of a change of heart, and united with the Protestant church at the time of its organization. He served the mission as teacher, and later as preacher, until his death and during a period of nearly fourteen years. The school was opened with ten scholars. The attendance soon increased to fifteen and twenty. The Armenians now called a council to determine what their relations to the mission and school should be. Their purpose in calling the meeting was to oppose the mission, but temperate councils prevailed, and they decided that it was most expedient neither to encourage nor to oppose the work. The Armenians were to some extent favorably influenced by a young merchant from Western Persia named Baron Matteos. He had been in prosperous circumstances and was of a wealthy family, but had suffered reverses in business. He had been converted through the preaching of Mr. Labaree. The social position and manners of this young man were such as to give weight to his words with many persons. He was quiet and gentlemanly, and gave evidence of a sincere faith. By identifying himself with the mission-work he incurred the ill-will of his own people. He and Baba rendered efficient service in the bookroom, which was in their care. Matteos in the next year returned to Tabriz, and was for some time in the service of the mission in that city. The Armenians now proposed a union of the two schools, on condition that no religious instruction should be given in it. Such a condition could not be accepted, and therefore the mission-school was continued. A large and influential number of this people are skeptics, but hold to the Church as a social organization essential to the perpetuity of the Armenian nation, language and literature. They desired to do much in the way of schools, but cared nothing for strictly religious doctrines and influences.

In the month of April the Shah departed for a tour of Europe. The event created great excitement. This was the first visit to European courts undertaken by any Shah, and was thought by many people to be ominous of evil. Farhaud Mirza, the governor of Ardelan, was called to the charge of affairs during the king's absence. The day of departure was fixed by favorable omens. The Sadr Azam, or prime minister, was the principal mover in the Shah's arrangements and in all the improvements going on in the kingdom and capital; but he brought down upon himself the displeasure of the mullahs and princes, and, most of all, the wrath of one of the king's wives, who was a great favorite of the king.

Prime Minister in Court Costume.   Page 103.

It is said that he opposed the wish of this woman to accompany the Shah to Europe, representing to the king that the woman would be an object of curiosity to Europeans, and by her costume would excite the mirth of the populace, which would be a dishonor to the queen and a source of mortification to the Shah. So the lady returned and occupied the palace at Neaveron, which is at the foot of Shimron. Here the mullahs and princes assembled during the king's absence and plotted the overthrow of the Sadr Azam. When the king returned to Anzile, he was there notified that the discharge of the Sadr Azam had been decreed, and that officer resigned, but was afterward appointed minister of foreign affairs. These events had their influence upon the court and populace, making them ill disposed toward foreigners. Some of the khans and their subordinates were insolent because they expected a restoration of the old order of the government.

The increase of the mission-school and the need of a place of worship made it necessary to construct a chapel, to be used also as a school-room. A small lot of land near the Casveen gate was purchased and a small building erected thereon. It was completed May 1st, and opened for services on the 9th of May. The Mohammedan workmen employed in constructing this chapel were very anxious to make a show of their own religion, knowing that the building was for Christians and thinking that their own fidelity to Islam might be questioned.

They were very careful to be seen at the hour of prayer, and therefore spread their garments upon which to kneel in the most public places by the side of the street and on the wall. The Sabbath services in this chapel were a Sabbath-school and preaching. These meetings were attended by Armenians, Jews and Mohammedans, and the room was filled to its utmost capacity. This good attendance continued until opposition was stirred up by the archbishop and some of his people, so that the Armenian attendants were fearful of suffering violence. The archbishop came from Julfa near Ispahan in the month of August. In his representations to the king he asked that the Armenians might not be made responsible for the acts of the Protestants, and represented that parties from America had come to Persia with a view to the conversion of Armenians and Mohammedans from the faiths of their fathers. In July three influential Armenians made complaint to the Naibe Sultan that the American missionary was endeavoring to subvert both the religion of the Armenians and of the Mohammedans. In consequence of this charge the naib sent a farash to the mission-school to see if there were any children of Mohammedans there. There were, however, no Mohammedan children in the school, and the farash so reported. Two children had been sent only a day or two before this, but, as the teacher was apprehensive of treachery, they were not received. Concerning the complaint about the conversion of Armenians, the naib is reported to have said, in substance, that since the missionaries teach the same Bible as that used by Armenians, it could not be said that they sought to destroy the Armenian religion. The mission was thus permitted to continue its work, but the order of the archbishop—for he had forbidden his people to attend the Protestant services of public worship—the opposition of the priest and the fear of Mohammedans reduced the number of attendants at the chapel to those who had virtually accepted Protestant sentiments and to the circle of their friends. The chapel was constructed as chapels are in America, with the front door opening on the street; but now the Armenians were so much alarmed, and so fearful of violence being offered by Mohammedans either at the instigation of the mullahs or at the suggestion of some of the Armenians, that they desired the front door might be permanently closed and an entrance made through the court. Their request was granted, and the front doorway was filled up with brick, and the vestibule used as a bookroom.

About twelve miles west of Tehran there was a village owned by Mohammedans and inhabited by both Armenians and Mussulmans. It was called Feruzbahrom and Zard Aub. The Armenians came to this place during the great famine, hoping to reap an ample harvest, for the adjacent lands are noted for their abundant supply of water and for fertility. The dwellings were miserable huts of sun-dried brick, having arched roofs of the same material. The wretched occupants of the village had perished of famine, and nearly every hut had fallen in part. About sixty Armenians now inhabited the broken hovels. They had no means of subsistence except such meagre aid as the owner of the village gave, to be repaid from the prospective harvest. The missionary and the colporteur Baba made frequent visits to this place, and established a congregation and school. Services were begun in January, and the school was opened in the month of May. All the villagers came to the meetings, and there was soon a marked change in them. They, as all Armenians are taught, believed that forgiveness of sins must be secured by the sacraments and absolution from a priest. They had no regard for the Sabbath as a holy day, and they did not hesitate to lie and cheat and swear. They now kept the Sabbath, and they were so alarmed at their state that some of them said, "There is nothing now that we fear so much as to lie and curse." The unhealthfulness of the place compelled them to seek a new home. A number died of fever, and nearly all were sick. In the selection of another village due regard was had to healthfulness, and they chose Bohmain in the Elburz Mountains and in the vicinity of Damavand. This village nestles among lofty mountains, and its adjacent fields are supplied with water from mountain-streams. The winters are severe, but in this place they have health and a fair measure of success in farming. In 1880 an effort was made by the mission in Tehran to establish a Protestant village where the adherents of the mission might enjoy the aid and advice of the missionaries without opposition. Owing to representations made of the fertility of the soil and the supply of water, the same locality was chosen, without knowledge or thought of the former experiences of the Armenians of that place. The sickness of all the people and the death of several in the course of the first year so disheartened the remnant that the project was abandoned. In the autumn of 1874, after the harvest had been gathered, the people of Feruzbahrom removed to Bohmain, where they have lived until the present time. As they passed through Tehran going to their new home, they lodged for a night in the mission-chapel, being excluded from the Armenian church by their affiliation with Protestants. In Bohmain they have had the care and aid of the mission in the way of schools and a preacher. Three years after their removal a converted priest was sent to reside with them.

Early in the summer there is an exodus of Europeans and native Persians from Tehran to the villages of Shimronaut. The missionary removed to the village of Vanak. This was the largest suburban settlement of Armenians. It is situated on a small plateau on the slope of Shimron. The site commands a view of the plain on the west and south, but the view of the city is obstructed by higher ground. Before the drought which preceded the famine of 1871–72 the place was supplied with water and gardens, but in the time of famine the trees were cut down and sold. Many of the people left for more favored regions. The remnant were kept alive by the funds distributed by foreigners and contributed from abroad. The British minister supported many by paying wages for workmen to construct roads. The funds contributed abroad were thus disbursed, and the refugees were employed in making roads to Gulak and Vanak. In the summer of 1873 there was but one garden near the village. It was just without the gate, and was owned by the aubdar of the Mustofe al Mamalake. Being, as the name denotes, the overseer of the water, he could obtain a supply for his garden. The place was hardly worthy the name "garden," for it had so suffered from drought that but few trees remained. This village was chosen by the missionary that he might have opportunity to labor for the Armenians who seemed to be specially inclined to give a favorable hearing. But the foreign Armenians of the city made a special effort to defeat his work. Money was given by them with which to open a school in the village. The son of the elder priest of the village was employed by them to teach. The two priests, Abraham and Megerditch, were incited to oppose the mission. The people were forbidden by them to visit the missionary or to attend the Protestant religious services. Priest Megerditch was stationed at the gateway to prevent the people from going to these services. Some of them, however, on one or two occasions left the village secretly, but on their return they were cursed and beaten by Megerditch. The feast-days were celebrated in the village with greater zest and expense than was usual. At such seasons the entire male population drink wine and arak to excess, the liquor being set out in large kettles and open jars in the courts of the houses and in the streets. In the fall the priest Abraham died and the charge fell to Megerditch. This man could hardly read the ritual, and could not read the Scriptures in the ancient language. Two years later he declared himself a Protestant. In the mean time, his wife had died, and by the laws of the Armenian Church he could not marry a second wife while a priest. He wished to marry again. His decision was considered a good indication by the mission, and was respected. He was admitted to the mission-school and training-class for young men. After having been in the school for several months he was sent to the Armenian settlement of Karaghan. Afterward, at his own request, he taught a small school in the village of Darooz, and finally was permitted to settle with his family in the village of Bohmain. Here he has remained until the present time, a consistent Christian and friend of the mission. Some of the prominent characteristics of this man disappeared at the time of his conversion. Before this he was a loud talker and a man of violent temper, but his subsequent life has been marked by great mildness and moderation. His wife and her father and mother were also of Vanak, and during many years. have been consistent members of the mission-church in Tehran.

As the season advanced the heat became intense. The irrigation of the fields in the early summer and the stretches of verdure lessened somewhat the degree of heat, but it was felt in greater intensity when the harvests were gathered and the irrigation of the land ceased. All the members of the missionary's family were prostrated with fever and were obliged to seek cooler air on Shimron. On this occasion the forethought exercised at the opening of the mission seemed to be timely, for medical attention was cheerfully rendered by Dr. Baker, medical superintendent of the government of India's telegraph corps in Persia. To have resided in the village occupied by the British legation would have given the missionary the pleasure of English society and have shortened the distance to be traveled by the physician; but the best interests of the work in hand seemed at the time to require that he should forego the pleasure and identify himself with the people for whom he came especially to labor.

Supervision of the congregation and the school near the Casveen gate required the missionary to reside in that part of the city. On returning, therefore, from Vanak, a house was rented in that quarter and near the chapel. The school for boys had been in session during the summer, and was now attended by forty pupils. The attendance at the school of the old Armenian church had risen from twenty-five to sixty scholars, a number of whom were admitted without charge. In fact, the school was now essentially a free school, thanks to competition with Protestant missions.

The interests of the work in Tehran required the missionary to attend the annual meeting of the Persian mission to be held in Oroomiah. Mr. Easton with his wife and Miss Jewett had been appointed to Tabriz, whither they had gone in the summer. Going by chapar to Tabriz, Mr. Bassett journeyed from that place to Oroomiah in company with Mr. Easton. At the village of Ola, near Salmas, they met one of the newly-appointed missionaries of the Basle society then on their way to Tabriz to open a mission of that society for the Nestorians. It was arranged at the meeting in Oroomiah that two colporteurs should go to Tehran for service in Eastern Persia, and that two native preachers should be sent to be located, one in Tehran and the other in Hamadan. Up to this time the school in Shevarin had been in charge of Ohanes, an Armenian of the village, and the work in Hamadan had been cared for by Mechail. Both of these young men had been in Oroomiah and in the school at Seir for a time, having been taken to that place by Mr. Shedd in 1869. The return of Mr. Bassett to Tehran could not be made before the 12th of December. The road was now covered with snow as far as to Sultaneah, a distance of nearly two hundred miles from Tabriz. The road for the greater part of the way lies over mountains and highlands. Violent rains prevailed along the valley of Tehran. In that city rain fell continuously during twelve days, and caused many roofs and houses to fall. There was not a dry ceiling to be seen in the city. The roofs of the best structures were found to be defective. The walls and roof of a chamber recently constructed over a part of the house occupied by the mission had fallen. The newly-made roof of earth, having become saturated with water, by its increased weight caused the main timbers to break, and in its fall carried the outer walls. Baba was sleeping in the room beneath, and was alarmed by the crash. He sprang from the bed just in time to avoid the heavy timber of the roof, which, crashing through the floor above him, fell into the bed from which but an instant before he had escaped. Most Persian houses are alike frail. If a stream of water strikes the unburned bricks of the walls, they dissolve at once. It is only by repeated sprinkling with straw and chaff, and frequent salting and rolling with a heavy stone roller, that the roofs can be kept in tolerable condition.

The distress in Hamadan caused by the famine of the previous year had not entirely ceased with the harvests of this year. Aid had been sent to the needy from the famine fund. Opposition had been excited against Mechail, and he had been assailed by Armenians and Mohammedans on various pretexts, especially on the charge of a misuse of the funds. The charge was thoroughly investigated, and it appeared to have been made on account of, and in revenge for, his refusal to comply with all the demands made upon him. The Mohammedans charged him with being an agent of foreigners. Some Armenians thought to harm the Protestant cause by injuring Mechail, for they knew him to be the most forward in the cause. A service was held, by permission of the priest Oracale, in the Armenian church. At the instigation of Mechail the handkerchiefs, crucifixes, crosses and paraphernalia of the old service were removed from the church, and tied up in a napkin and put away in the house of a priest, where they have remained. The entire community had become convinced of the error of the old forms of worship and demanded a reformation. A few persons yet held to the old service, and the priest yet officiated for their benefit. Personal interest seemed to lead him to pursue a compromising course, whereby he hoped to keep the favor of the archbishop and his own flock. So long as he saw his own support to be assured he was quite willing that his people should take their own course. He seemed to have felt some distrust of the old order, and at heart to have entertained kind feelings toward Protestant sentiments. He pursued this policy until the last. A successor has never been appointed, or if appointed has never been able to recover the lost ground. Mechail was not an ordained preacher. His zeal could not prevent the effects of some imprudence on his part. He was naturally progressive and aggressive, and the same spirit which impelled him in these first days of reformation now leads him to argue with the missionaries that the native Protestant Christians can manage the missionary work more economically and efficiently than the missionaries themselves.

The same methods were adopted to make Mechail's position untenable which are so common in like conditions. The Mohammedan authorities were set upon him, and their subordinates endeavored to extort money. He was obliged to leave the place, and he fled to Tehran. Here he was given charge of the bookstall in the bazar, with the privilege of laboring as he had opportunity among his people. At times he was appointed to preach, and was given charge of the chapel, but he did not succeed in holding an Armenian congregation any great length of time. A congregation gathered by the missionary was sure to run down on his hands, notwithstanding the fact that he had a fluent use of the Armenian tongue. The only worker in Hamadan during several months next succeeding these events was the young teacher of Shevarin. A little later Mirza Abraham reopened the school in the city, and held the place with fair success as teacher during several years and until his death. He was an Armenian of Hamadan, a member of the Protestant church organized a few years later than these events, but he had been instructed in the schools of Hamadan only.

Mechail and his Wife. Page 117.

The Nestorian preacher who had been appointed by the annual meeting to go to Hamadan, and who was ordained for this purpose, concluded to remain on the plain of Oroomiah. The deacons Guergues and Babilla came on to Tehran as previously arranged. Their journey was made in the month of January, 1874, the most unfavorable season of the year for travel, but the time was of their own choosing. The road was covered with deep snows and the way was blocked for some days by heavy storms. Owing to the unfavorable season, the two deacons were permitted to remain in Tehran until the spring. Guergues had formerly been in charge of the bookroom in Tehran. As soon as the roads were passable, he went on to Hamadan, arriving in that city in April. Mechail and Babilla went with books to the villages of Karaghan and Hamadan.

CHAPTER VI.

Persecution in Tabriz—Nestorian Helpers—Tour of Mr. Coan—Petition of Nestorians—How Disposed of—Mr. Bruce in Julfa—Opening of School for Girls—Supply of Books—Proposed Distribution of Scriptures in Khorasan—The City of Yezd—Situation and People—Departure and Tour of Mechail and Babilla—Reception in Yezd—Summoned by the Mujtaheed—Peril—Interposition of the Governor—Flight of the Colporteurs—Results—Transfer of Native Assistants—Opening of School in the Eastern Quarter—Intemperance—Summer Retreat at Tajreesh—Environments—Persian Monogamy—Religious Services—Affairs in Hamadan and Shevarin—Mission Removed to North Side of Tehran, called Shimron Gate—Description of Buildings—Removal of Girls' School—Training-Class—Course of Study—Summary of Schools—Annual Meeting in Tabriz—Arrival of Mr. Potter—Return to Tehran—Work of Mr. Potter—Affairs in Shevarin and Hamadan—Tour to Hamadan—The Governor, Interview with—Trial of the Kathoda—Intemperance of the Native Persian Armenians—The Kashish Khanah—Ceremonies of the Khanah Described—The Khanah Suppressed—Taxes Relevied—Priest Oracale seeks a Remission of the Taxes—Negotiations with the Mustofe—The Priest Presents a Petition to the Shah—Teachers sent to Karaghan and Rasht—Summer Retreat—Ascent of Shimron—Reinforcements—Mr. Bassett's Tour to Tiflis—Rasht, Armenian Congregations in—Sketch of Mission-Work and Results in Rasht—Baku—Armenian Congregation of Protestants—Armenian Priest—Armenians of Shamakha—Sargis, his Work and Character—Detention of Reinforcements—Mission- and Bible-Work in Tiflis—Russian Sabbath—Departure of Missionaries to their Respective Fields—Miss Sarah Bassett takes Charge of the Girls' School—

Christian Literature in Persian—Condition of the Persian Scriptures—New Edition of Scriptures Sought—Mr. Wright and the British and Foreign Bible Society—Persian Hymns and Music—Attendance of Jews—Request for Jewish School—Sketch of Jewish School.

IN February of 1874 there was a sore persecution of the Mohammedans of Tabriz who were suspected of Christian sentiments. Information of the fact having come to Tehran by telegraph, the missionary in that city caused notice to be sent to the Mohammedans known to be attendants at the religious services, in order that they might absent themselves from the chapel for a time. The precaution, however, seemed to be unnecessary, as no attempt was made by the mullahs to do violence to any one.

All the Nestorian preachers engaged for Tehran by the mission in Oroomiah failed to come. Deacons Elea and Shamoon remained in the western field. Priest Mosha came as far as Tabriz and entered the service of the mission in that city, being engaged to do so by Mr. Easton and Mr. Coan. The latter, in view of his intended return to America, had arranged for a tour to Tehran and Ispahan. He left Tabriz in the month of March, going thence by chapar to the capital. The roads were in a bad state, owing to the rains and melting snow. Remaining a few days in Tehran, he in company with Mr. Bassett went by chapar to Ispahan, reaching that place in three days, on the 18th of April. They returned to Tehran on the 7th of May. Mr. Coan had special requests to make of the Persian authorities. These were embodied in a petition which was sent from the evangelical Nestorians, and which reached the capital after his departure. The objects named in the petition were—the release of the Nestorians who had been drafted to serve in the army as musicians; the prevention of extortion practiced on Nestorians returning from Russia; relief from the violence perpetrated by the khans in the villages; relief from the exactions of the sarparast; and last, though not least, the recognition of the "Evangelical Nestorian Church" as a separate organization having all the rights of other recognized sects, and having an agent resident at the court of the Shah with power to hear complaints and to refer matters to the Shah. On consultation in Tehran the last object was thought to be undesirable and opposed to the best interests of the mission-work among all the sects of Persia, and was therefore abandoned. The usually slow progress of affairs in Persia prevented the authorities from giving attention at this time to the other objects named. The formal and written petition had not yet come to hand. These matters, therefore, were left with the British minister. Soon after this the sarparast died, and this made any reference to his administration unnecessary. The minister interposed in behalf of the musicians. He was told by the Persian minister of foreign affairs that the young men would be permitted to return to Oroomiah on furlough, and that they would not again be called out. At the expiration of several months they returned to their homes. It should be noted here that non-Mohammedans are not required to render military service, but are taxed in lieu of such service. It was thought, therefore, to be unlawful and oppressive to compel Nestorians to enter the army in any capacity.

It had been proposed that the American mission should occupy Julfa in case the Church Missionary Society should not do so. Mr. Bruce was now living in Julfa carrying on independent missionary work. It was undecided whether he would remain longer than might be necessary to complete his revision of the New Testament. An officer of that society had stated to a member of the American mission that his society would not undertake work in Persia. However, a few months later the mission of Mr. Bruce was adopted by the Church Missionary Society as its own mission. Here, again, as in case of the Romanists, competition seems to have had a salutary effect. There being no post between Ispahan and Hamadan, it was found to be most expeditious for Mr. Coan to return to Tehran. He journeyed thence to Oroomiah *via* Hamadan and Senah.

A day-school for girls was opened in Tehran on the 24th of April with twelve pupils. Schools were reopened in the villages of Feruzbahrom and Darooz— the former for the benefit of the Mohammedans and a few families of Armenians yet living there who could not leave the village at that time.

One of the most important departments of mission-work is the circulation by sale or gift of Christian books, especially the Scriptures. These books are required to be in nearly all the languages spoken in the kingdom. They were in Persian, Armenian, Turkish and Hebrew. The sources of supply were the Bible and tract societies. They were obtained chiefly from the American agencies in Constantinople. The books were conveyed by caravan from Trebizond to Tehran. The British and Foreign Bible Society was the only publisher of the Scriptures in Persian. The Religious Tract Society of London very generously responded to calls for religious books in Persian, so far as any were extant in that language. No printing in Persian was done by any American society, but books in that language, especially the Scriptures, were obtained in great part from Dr. Bliss, the agent of the American Bible Society in Constantinople. The books, especially the text-books prepared for schools in the Armenian tongue, were much admired by the Persians for the excellent style in which they were gotten up.

Two years previous to this time a proposition had been made by Mr. Arthington of Leeds, England, that two colporteurs should be sent from Tehran through Khorasan *viâ* Yezd and Tubbes in the great desert, thence to return to the capital, the object of the tour to be the distribution of the Gospels of Luke and John in the Persian. These Gospels had not been published in separate volumes, but, at the suggestion of Mr. Labaree of Oroomiah, the American Bible Society, by its agent in Constantinople, arranged for the publication of these Gospels by the British and Foreign Bible Society, and the work of their distribution, according to the plan proposed, so far as practicable was committed to the supervision of the missionary appointed to Tehran. The books reached that city some two years later, and arrangements were made for their distribution. Mechail and Babilla having completed their work in the Karaghan district, and having returned to Tehran, were quite willing to go to Yezd on the proposed tour. It was suggested that they should go at once to Yezd, open a bookstall there and go on immediately to Mashhad.

The city of Yezd is situated in the desert of Khorasan, but is surrounded by a small tract of some fertility. It is reputed to have a population of thirty thousand souls; all are Mohammedans except about five thousand Guebers and fifteen hundred or two thousand Jews. The place is distinguished for its manufacture of cotton, silk and woolen goods, as well as for its colony of Guebers. Of the colony of Jews, four hundred perished in the late famine. We have no record of the mortality from the same cause among the Guebers.

Having taken a stock of Scriptures in Persian and Hebrew, and having been charged to "salute no man by the way," the two colporteurs set out for Yezd on the 18th of May, 1874. They went to Kashan, and thence crossed the section of the desert which intervenes between

Kashan and Yezd. This part of the way is very dreary. The stations consist each of a post-house and a few huts. They were very glad to have company by the way, and so found a traveler like themselves bound for the chief city of the desert. They told him of their purpose and work. When they had gone over the greater part of the distance their traveling companion wished to hasten on, and as he carried no impediments in the way of books he could travel faster than they could, and as he had reached the settlements near Yezd, he had no special need of any protection which their company could afford. Before leaving them he advised them as to the caravansary they should occupy.

On arriving in Yezd the colporteurs found that their coming had been made known. Their companion had reported with the view of preparing the way for them, and had added such embellishments as an Oriental only knows how to use. He sought, no doubt, to do a good turn to the colporteurs. The people came in large numbers to the caravansary, and there was a decided run in the book business. But many persons came out of curiosity. The business was reported to the principal mujtaheed, and he sent his farashes to bring the young men to his presence. This put a serious aspect upon the situation, for the mujtaheeds are known to be zealous guardians of the laws of Islam, and not at all disposed to tolerate Christian books. The summons was alarming, yet the colporteurs obeyed. The mujtaheed received them very coolly and declared the New Testament to be a lie. He then demanded that they should become Mussulmans or convince him so thoroughly of the truth of the Bible that he should be constrained to become a Christian. This is the usual prelude to violent acts on the part of a Mohammedan mullah. As he may resort to force, he has the conclusive argument. The mujtaheed ordered that Mussulmans should return the Scriptures purchased. The populace reflected the sentiments of the religious authorities. Some of the people attempted to stone the young men. These were so fearful of violence being offered that they did not dare to lodge in the caravansary, but remained at night in the gardens without. The governor of the city, however, was very friendly. He sent word to the mujtaheed that as these men were in the service of foreigners, their case fell under the jurisdiction of the secular authorities and minister of foreign affairs. Having heard from the colporteurs a statement of their affairs, he advised them to leave the city, owing to the evident evil design of the mujtaheed. They dared not leave the city by day, but withdrew in the night to the open fields near by and departed at early dawn for Ispahan. All their books, however, were sold, and the supply was wholly inadequate to the demand. We may reasonably believe that great good was done. The word was brought openly to light in one of the darkest places of Asia. The reception given to the Bible was owing, in great part, we may suppose, to the fact that the book had not before this been openly distributed in Yezd, nor had missionary work been attempted there.

From Ispahan the colporteurs returned to Tehran in the month of July. In the following month Babilla was sent to Hamadan to take the place of Guergues, as the latter wished to return to Oroomiah. He was willing to remain in the capital a few months, and was given charge of the chapel on the west side of town. A school was opened in the Armenian colony in the eastern quarter of the city, and religious services were held here on Sabbaths. There was not a house in the colony in which wine or arak was not made, and the missionary stipulated in renting the room that no wine or alcohol should be made or drunk on the premises. Every house was a drinking-den to which Mohammedans resorted for gambling and drinking. The manufacture and sale of alcoholic drinks is the most lucrative business in which the non-Mohammedans can engage: it could not be so profitable were there no Mussulman patrons.

The season was far advanced before the missionary removed for the summer. The village of Tajreesh was selected for the summer retreat. It is the largest village of Shimronaut, and contains about five thousand people, all of whom are Mohammedans. It is some two miles above and north of the British and Russian retreats. A good supply of water, arable lands and a high altitude have all combined to make this the most desirable

Apartments of the King's Treasurer.

Page 129.

suburban village. It is surrounded by extensive gardens and groves of poplar, fruit and chinar trees. Many of the officers of the Persian government have their retreats here. The French legation occupies spacious grounds in the border of the village, and the Austrians for some time rented premises a short distance below the French. The village itself is a cluster of miserable hovels of Persian peasants, but it commands an extensive prospect of the plains on the south. The city, however, is hidden by low hills at the foot of Shimron. During the summer religious services were held on Sabbaths in the building occupied by the mission, and were attended by Armenians from the villages of Darooz and Vanak and by Mohammedans and Europeans. The garden and pavilion of Farhaud Mirza were adjacent to the premises occupied by the mission. Mrs. Bassett was occasionally a guest of the Persian ladies of the prince's household. The prince had but one wife, in deference, it is said, to the lady's family; so also his daughter was the only wife of a prince. It is frequently the case that a Persian will forego the privilege of polygamy out of regard to the rank of his wife or from affection for her. This fact shows the popular judgment of the relation of polygamy as an institution to the women of Persia.

A little way from the mission-premises was the garden of the king's treasurer and the king's son-in-law. The summer palace of this prince was on an extensive scale, and the grounds were spacious and were laid out in good taste. The owner of the property was suddenly killed while the palace was yet incomplete, and it remains in about the same condition as that in which he left it. Yet the place is not so incomplete as to be unworthy of the pretentious name which it bears—namely, Boghe Firdose, the "Garden of Heaven." This prince also had but one wife, for it was thought to be wholly unworthy and unbecoming his connection with the king for him to take another.

At this time there was no marked change in the affairs of the mission in Hamadan. The priest of Shevarin professed great friendship for the mission, and desired to have a school in that village. He was very friendly so long as his own son was employed as teacher and he practiced the old rites of the Church and taught the Church Catechism. This book is a curious work when considered in the light of Protestant sentiment. On visiting the school in the next spring the missionary observed that the catechism was taught, and he requested the children to recite it. In answer to the question, "What evidence do you give of being a Christian?" the reply was made, "I make the sign of the cross and take the sacrament." The old priest would not tolerate any other teaching, and finally became so hostile as to incite the people against the school and the Protestant worship. Ohanes was put in charge of the school, but in the course of the winter he was driven from the place by the kathoda of the village and the school was closed.

Girls' School, Tehran.

There was now a promise of reinforcements from the United States for the mission, and it seemed to be important to obtain premises adapted to the prospective increase of the mission-work. Buildings were to be had in the northern part of the city at a reasonable rental, and arrangements were therefore made to secure them with a view to their occupancy in the autumn. The place was situated near the king's garden, Lala Zar, and between it and what is now the Tob Maidon. The buildings were not all that could be desired, but they were ample. They were divided by four courts, each of which could be entirely separated from the others. One of the divisions was appropriated to the use of the girls' school, and the rooms were furnished after the Persian fashion. This school had been opened in the house of an Armenian woman named Anna Haunum, near the old Armenian church, in the western part of town. The school was kept as a day-school during the summer. On the 8th of February, 1875, it was removed to the new quarters provided for it, and was opened as a boarding-school with nine pupils. On the 22d of the month the attendance had increased to fifteen boarders and two day pupils, under the supervision of Mrs. Abigail W. Bassett and Mr. Bassett. The instruction was in charge of Mirza Mechail, and later was in the care of an Armenian of Tehran named Ohanes. A native woman had charge of the domestic arrangements, subject to the direction of the missionaries. The rooms of another part of the mission-premises were used for recitation by a class of young men who were preparing to be teachers and preachers. The class numbered seven persons, all of whom, except one, were from Hamadan. All of them became members of the church, and have led consistent Christian lives, and four of them are preachers in the service of the mission, three being in Tehran and its vicinity and one in Hamadan. Two of the class were sent to Roberts College at Constantinople in 1883, and after remaining there three years they returned to Tehran, where they are now employed as teachers. One of the class is in Hamadan, and is said by the missionaries of that city to be an efficient man and preacher. He has doubtless been greatly helped by the training and experience obtained in Hamadan. These young men at this time pursued their studies in Armenian under the instruction of Lazar, who was considered the best scholar in ancient Armenian to be had in Tehran. They took lessons in Persian and Arabic from a well-qualified Persian, and they received instruction every day in the Bible and in Christian doctrine from the missionary. A large room in the building occupied by the mission was used for the services of public worship, and the missionary preached here every Sabbath for the benefit of the pupils of that school and the people living in that part of the town. There were now three schools in Tehran and one in the village of Darooz.

Armenians and Mohammedans gathered frequently in

Training-class of Young Men.

the book-room in the bazar for conversation with the native helpers and other Christians. There were also frequent visits of inquirers at the mission-premises. The number of scholars in the east-side school was now seventeen, in the west-side school thirty, and in the girls' school seventeen—making, in all the schools of the city, sixty-four pupils.

The annual meeting of the Persian mission was this year to be held in the city of Tabriz, and it was necessary that the missionary at Tehran should attend the meeting. He therefore journeyed to that city by chapar, this being the fifth time that he had made the journey between the cities of Tehran and Tabriz. The mission recommended at this time an appropriation for the purchase of press and type by the station of Tehran for printing in Persian. The purchase of the press was made four years later. As previously arranged by letter, the missionary here met the Rev. Joseph L. Potter, who had been appointed to the mission in Tehran. Mr. Potter came from the United States by way of Constantinople, Trebizond and Van. At the close of the meeting the two missionaries journeyed to Tehran, reaching that city on the 21st of November, 1874. During the winter Mr. Potter gave his attention to the study of the Persian language, assisted in the secular business of the mission and preached in English to a congregation of foreigners now gathered for Sabbath services in the mission-premises. A large reception-room in these premises furnished ample and comfortable quarters for the services of public worship.

The work in Hamadan demanded attention, and early in the spring the missionaries visited that city. The opposition to the mission-work in the village of Shevarin has been mentioned. There was a division in the village between the adherents of the old Church and the advocates of reform. Opposition was being stirred up in Hamadan also. The governor of the city at this time was a brother of the Shah. He had represented Persia at foreign courts, and was a gentleman of refined manners and well informed in European affairs. It is a significant fact that he takes European and American periodicals. Courtesy required that the missionaries should call upon him. At the appointed hour they went to the palace. It was late in the afternoon and after the usual crowd of the dewan khanah had been dismissed. The prince had retired to his private apartments. The missionaries were conducted through a labyrinth of corridors and rooms. Such an approach may be well calculated to impress the mind of an Oriental with an idea of the sanctity of the person who dwells within, but no such impression is made on the mind of one accustomed to Western ideas of business and the value of men. It is not to be assumed, however, that Western ideas are necessarily better than those of the East in this particular. In Europe and America the common estimate of men is affected very much by the

Governor of Hamadan.

extent of the lands through which the house is approached or by the extent of the factory and quantity of machinery in view of which one passes to the man who controls the establishment. The Asiatic has not yet formed his estimate by this measure.

The prince entered the room wearing a cashmere gown trimmed with fur and reaching to the instep, and embroidered Persian slippers of Rasht work. He resembles the Shah in stature and features. The room was furnished with a Persian carpet, curtains and chairs. Reference was made to the conduct of the kathoda of Shevarin in reply to the question of the governor if there was anything he could do for us. We asked if there was not liberty for Armenians in religious matters, to which he replied, "Yes, there is religious liberty for everybody in Persia." The kathoda and priest had professed to act in obedience to the orders of the archbishop. The governor advised that we refer the matter to the prince, an officer of the Tehran government, who owned the village, saying that if this person did not attend to the business he would himself see to it. The conduct of the kathoda was referred to the prince, and a hearing of the case was appointed. The kathoda had threatened Protestants, and had said that if they continued their efforts "blood would be shed." The prince expressed doubts at first whether the case did not fall within the jurisdiction of the archbishop as the head and ecclesiastical ruler of the Armenians. To this it was replied that the mission did not recognize the authority of the archbishop, and that it rested with the authorities of the secular law to say whether any persons in Persia had the right or privilege of changing their religious faith and worship. Christians, Jews and Guebers were permitted to become Mohammedans, and it was understood by the mission that the religious liberty of these sects was recognized by the Persian authorities, and examples were cited, as in Tehran, Oroomiah, Ispahan and other places. To this view of the case the prince assented, saying that if any of the people of Shevarin desired a school or to hold religious services they ought not to be prevented. The result was that the prince ordered the kathoda to be bastinadoed then and there. The missionaries, however, had no desire to see the man harmed, and at their request he was discharged on promising never again to interfere with the schools and congregation and on giving bonds to keep the peace. The prince inquired, "What shall be done with the priest?" He deserved to be turned out of the village, as he had driven the Protestant teacher away, but the missionaries not wishing to retaliate, he was permitted to remain in the village. Unfortunately, in this case the teacher was intemperate. This fact was no real apology for the conduct of the priest and kathoda, nor was it any cause of their action, for they also drank.

The complaint against the teacher was started at this time, because of the known temperance sentiments of

Armenian Priest.   Page 145.

the mission, it being said that he did not represent the mission. It may have been thought to have some influence with Mohammedans by such a charge, yet it could not have much weight with them, for the habits of all the Armenians were too well known to them. When the missionary, in the presence of the prince, said to the kathoda, "How can you, who drink and are drunken, make such a complaint of this teacher?" he could only reply, "We are drunken in the *night*, but this man is drunk in the *daytime*." The teacher reconciled all parties, however, on the temperance question by signing a total-abstinence pledge. At this stage of the mission-work it was impossible to find Armenians of strictly temperate habits. All non-Mohammedans are in the habit of drinking wine or arak, usually both. While they extol temperance in sentiment, they think it no sin to drink. Priests and people, therefore, use wine to beastly excess. We cannot expect them to become advocates of temperance until they have been instructed and reformed. But it is a marvel to what excess of drunkenness they will go in secret. Drunkenness by day is one of the great improprieties. Such is the force of this custom that intemperance practiced during many years is often concealed.

Guergues and Babilla having left Hamadan, Caspar, of the training-class, was appointed a temporary supply of the congregation. Some of the people had opened the Kashish Khanah, so called by Armenians, but Falgier

Khanah, as named by Mohammedans and Jews; that is, "house of magic art." The literal translation of the first name is "priest's house," so named, it is said, because first opened by a priest. The writer once held a conversation with a man who had charge of the Kashish Khanah during several years. The ceremonies practiced in the place were simply the repetition of selections from the New Testament and ritual and other sacred books for the cure of the sick and for other objects. An extensive business was carried on in this house in writing the passages of the Bible and the prayers on parchment and paper, to be used as talismans and to be laid on the sick. Mohammedans were the patrons of the establishment. When asked if he thought the business was right, he said that he did so consider it at the time. When asked if he knew of any cures of diseases being effected by the ceremonies and prayers, he replied that he did. He justified the traffic carried on by saying that there could be no harm in reading the Bible to the people and reading or reciting prayers for them. He justified the sale of the talismans by the financial straits of the colony and the exactions of the Persian authorities. The Mohammedans, he said, filched from Christians, and to take advantage of them in return is, he argued, entirely justifiable.

Whatever the fact may be as to the efficacy of these prayer-houses, it is certain that some of the people have great faith in them. But many resort to them in des-

Armenian Patriarch.   Page 149.

peration as an expedient in emergencies. The missionary had required that the Kashish Khanah should be closed, but there were some persons in the colony who yet adhered to the old order of things or acted independently. The matter having now been considered with the people, the missionaries informed the priest Oracale and the congregation that the mission would withdraw from them entirely unless the khanah were abandoned. They therefore gave a written agreement not to open the institution again, and that should any one do so he should be excluded from the congregation. Matters in Hamadan and Shevarin having been adjusted as far as seemed to be possible at this time, the missionaries returned to Tehran.

In the course of a few months after the events recorded above the Persian authorities relevied the old tax of two hundred and six tomans on the Armenians, and the colonists were not able to pay it. This tax had been levied many years before under an assessment made when the colony numbered one hundred houses of some seven hundred souls, but the colony now comprised no more than thirty houses, or about two hundred souls at the most. Priest Oracale came to Tehran for the purpose of getting the tax remitted. The priest remained in Tehran during several months. The secretary named Mustofe al Mamalake had charge of the assessments, but he committed the business to subordinates, who resorted to all manner of expedients to extort from the people. The mustofe finally agreed to obtain a firman from the Shah remitting the whole tax, provided he were paid the equivalent of the tax for one year and twelve hundred bottles of wine. The sum of money was finally discounted to one hundred tomans, the amount paid and the firman issued to be delivered on receipt by the mustofe of twelve hundred bottles of wine. These were afterward sent from Hamadan, and the firman obtained. Since that time the Armenians have been free from the oppressive tax.

There was a curious incident connected with this affair. It is a custom with the Shah to permit the presentation of petitions to himself as he passes through the streets. This is made possible by the order of escort which is adopted. In that order there is a long space between the van- and rear-guards. In this space the Shah rides or walks alone. Footmen called shahteers—that is, spears of the king—walk on the highway on either hand of the Shah, separated by wide spaces. A person wishing to present a petition stands with his paper on his bare head and close by the road where the Shah will see him. The priest of Hamadan, having become weary with delays, concluded to try a petition, and so stood in the highway. He wore, as usual, his black gown, and, uncovering his head, placed the paper on it. He was seen by the king, who after inquiring of a shahteer who the man was, ordered the petition to be received. The petition was for the relief of the congregation from the taxes. The Shah wrote on the back of the paper this order to the mustofe: viz. "Examine the taxes of the Armenians of Hamadan and report to me." Nothing further was heard until the above-mentioned proposal of that officer. The taxes were remitted for this year, but in the following year were again demanded, the reason assigned being that the wine had not been delivered. It was forthwith forwarded to the mustofe.

At the close of the school-year young men of the training-class were sent as colporteurs to Karaghan and to Rasht. Earnest requests for schools and teachers had been received from both these places. From the former place the request first came in 1873, but the increased work and expense could not then be undertaken. The summer retreat this season was the village of Tajreesh, but the house rented was the only one that could be obtained. It was on the margin of the village, and so exposed on the north and east to the heat of barren lands as to become in the course of the summer extremely hot, although the altitude of the mountain at this point is not less than five thousand feet above the sea.

Some account of a day of recreation in the mission may be a pleasant episode in our narrative. The two missionaries set out for the ascent of Shimron. The mountain is very precipitous, yet a road has been constructed by which beasts of burden pass very near the summit. "Starting," writes Mr. Bassett, "at dawn, August 19th, we followed the road by Sayedabad. From this place there is no more than a blind trail of goatherds. We led our horses over the greater part of the ascent. In some places the rocks seemed to be impassable, but by a zigzag course we picked our way over the huge rocks and up the steep sides of the ravines. Having been told that there is a glacier on the northern slope of the mountain, we passed below the highest point, going to the opposite side; but we found no more than a few drifts of snow in the shaded places. Not a plant or a shrub grew on the mountain-side. Patches of green grass were seen in places where the snow had recently melted. The highest point of snow was found to be 11,950 feet above the sea-level. Near this point we ate our luncheon, and Mr. Potter noted that water boiled at 189° Fahrenheit. We began to return by crossing the highest point, now covered with sunlight and clear of snow, and found that my barometer indicated an altitude of 12,750 feet. From this summit we had a fine view of the mountains on the north and of the gorges or valleys of the Shah Rud and Jorje Rud. On the south were the mountains of Karaghan and broad stretches of the desert and country toward Koom. At our feet were the plains of Ra and Tehran and the city nine thousand two hundred and fifty feet below us."

Word having been received of the arrival at Constantinople of reinforcements for the mission, it was arranged that Mr. Bassett should go to Tiflis to meet those persons of the party who had been appointed to Tehran. This seemed to be necessary, for the route through Georgia and Persia is difficult to one who has not a knowledge of the languages spoken in those countries or who is not acquainted with the mode of travel customary in them, and an escort is indispensable to ladies unaccustomed to the country. The missionary left the capital on the 24th of September, 1875, going *viâ* Rasht and Baku, the most direct route to the capital of Georgia. The road to Rasht crosses the plains of Tehran and Casveen and the Elburz Mountains, and passes through the jungle of Gelan, a distance of twenty-five miles. Rasht is the principal emporium of the Caspian sea-coast in Persia, but the seaport is about eighteen miles north-westward of that city and on the northern side of the bay called Mord Aub. While in Rasht opportunity was given the missionary to investigate the condition of the Armenians and to consider the expediency of opening mission-work here. Religious services were held in the house of an Armenian named Zohrab. The two young men from Tehran had opened a school. One of them gave his attention to colportage. The Armenians had no school, but soon after this began one in the house of the priest. It was started in opposition to the mission effort. The priest opposed the Protestants from the first. He had been abroad in Europe for the purpose of obtaining funds wherewith to complete the two churches under his care, one in Rasht and the other in Anzile. The walls of both structures were nearly completed, but work had ceased for lack of funds. These were obtained, however, in a year or two, and the structures finished.

The mission-work begun in Rasht at this time has been continued until the present day. It was interrupted in 1876, but resumed in the following year. It was again suspended by reason of the plague. Mechail was living here with his family when the plague first appeared, and he thereupon returned to Tehran. This scourge was attended with great mortality, but fortunately was not communicated to any other city in the kingdom. In the autumn of 1883 a church was organized in Rasht, and has been sustained, and supplied with native teachers and preachers from Tehran. The organization of the church was the immediate result of the labors of Mirza Lazar, the first teacher in Tehran. He taught and preached in Rasht in 1881–82, with much efficiency and acceptance. It has been difficult to find native Persians of other places who are willing to live in Rasht as teachers and preachers, owing to the unhealthfulness of the Caspian Sea coast.

The missionary continued his journey by steamer to Baku. Arriving at this place on Sabbath morning, he went immediately to the place of worship of the Protestant congregation. He had been informed of this society by an Armenian whom he met in Rasht, and who was a passenger on the steamer. The people were now assembled for worship, and were led by Avek Vartinoff,

an Armenian and member of the police. Making himself known to this man, he addressed the people, and an appointment was made for him to preach in the afternoon. The congregation met in a private house, having no place or house of worship. It was understood that the Russian authorities would not permit the erection of a church by this society, the organization not being recognized by them. There was a marked contrast between the appearance of the Armenians of this place and their coreligionists of Persia. The former seemed to be in much better circumstances than the latter. This contrast may be observed in all the Armenians of Russia. By invitation the missionary dined with the priest of one of the principal Armenian churches of Baku. This man in the early years of his priesthood had professed Protestant sentiments and went to Germany, entering the service of the German missionaries; but the privations to be met were much greater than he had anticipated, and he returned to the service of the Armenian Church. A pleasant and tidy family gathered at the table over which the priest and his wife presided after the customs of Europeans. Arriving at Shamakha, the missionary met the leader of the Protestant Armenians of that place. The mission of Sargis has been aided by the Germans with funds for the erection of buildings and support of schools and teachers. The pastor of this flock is now an old man, and is disposed to retire from the active duties of his charge. He is in many particulars a remarkable man—remarkable for his piety, intellect, self-sacrifice and achievements. His life has been one of trial and exciting emergencies, and the work he has accomplished is an example to all his people who would benefit their race. Considering the work to which he has been called, it seems to have been fortunate that he has chosen a celibate life.

On arriving at Tiflis the missionary received word of the detention of the reinforcements at Constantinople on account of the sickness of a son of Mr. Labaree. It was arranged, however, that the other members of the party should come on to Tiflis, and thence go on to Persia. A week must elapse before they could get to Pote. During this time the missionary made the acquaintance of some of the Armenians and Nestorians of that city. There was but a small band of the latter people. The Armenians of Tiflis are many and prosperous, but no Protestant mission has been opened among them, owing to the restrictions put on such effort by the Russian government. The British and Foreign Bible Society has sustained a dépôt of its publications and an agent here. Mr. Watt was the successful agent of that society at this time. He had sold many thousand copies of the Scriptures to the soldiers of the Russian army. The missionary was much impressed with the absence of Sabbath observance in Russia. The Sabbath is the great market-day, and from this circumstance has come the Turkish and Mohammedan name of the Christian Sab-

Baku Mussulman and Wife.   Page 161.

bath; that is, Bazar Guen, market-day. The churches were opened for worship and the shops for trade. The entire contents of the shops appeared to have been turned into the streets. The highways were blocked with loads of wood, provender, vegetables, furniture, clothing and everything that market-men and merchants have to sell or that people are supposed to want.

The party from Constantinople having come to Pote and Tiflis at the appointed time, arrangements were made for the journey to Persia. Mr. Stocking had now come from Oroomiah, and accompanied Miss Van Duzee and Miss Pogue to that city to engage in the mission-work there. Miss Sarah Bassett having been appointed to the mission in Tehran, she, in company with her uncle, journeyed to that city, where they arrived in the month of December. She immediately took charge of the girls' school, making her home in the building occupied by the pupils. Though not then acquainted with the Armenian language, she was able to superintend the business and domestic arrangements of the school, and in the course of the following year was able to superintend the instruction in the Armenian language.

One of the most seriously-felt wants at this time was a Christian literature in Persian. There were almost no published works in that tongue to use as text-books or with which to supplement the teaching of the missionaries. There was much in the Armenian that was available for Armenians. The books prepared in

Constantinople, though differing somewhat from the vernacular of Persian Armenians, are fairly well understood by this people. But in the Persian language there is no trace of Christian literature, except the few books which have been prepared within the last fifty years, which may all be counted on one's fingers. Martyn's translation of the New Testament and Glen's version of the Old Testament are the ones commonly used. Attention was given to the form of the Persian Scriptures by the missionaries in Tehran. The only edition of the Old Testament was an octavo volume of 1658 pages. The New Testament was an octavo volume of 532 pages, and the entire Bible was made up of these two bound in one volume of 2190 octavo pages. The great size of the book was a serious obstacle to the general circulation and use of it. The members of the Tehran mission recommended (February 25, 1876) to the British and Foreign Bible Society that it issue an edition of the entire Scriptures in Persian in a small form suitable for general circulation. The recommendation was adopted by that society, and as soon as practicable thereafter such an edition was published. Rev. William Wright, the superintendent of publication of the society, responded promptly to the request of the mission, and was ever ready to encourage the work of Bible distribution in Persia. The Bible-work in that land owes much to his encouragement and efficient aid, sustained by the noble society which he represents. The whole-souled and manly spirit which that society by its officers exercises toward the weary workers in desert and dreary lands is truly refreshing.

A small collection of translated hymns, prepared at first by Deacon Yohannan in Tehran in 1874, having been revised and enlarged by Mr. Bassett, was now published at a Mohammedan press in Tehran (March, 1876) for the use of the mission. This appears to be the first and only collection of Christian hymns in the Persian. A few hymns were translated and added by Mr. Bassett in 1884. This little book has been used in the services of public worship since the time of the first edition until now. The preparation of sacred song for worship in Persian is one of the most difficult of tasks. Persians have no music which can be used in religious services. In fact, they have no music at all which is not an importation. The music of the Armenian Church is no more than reading and intoning. The Mohammedans have a method of chanting a few well-known pieces, but these are unwritten and are not suitable to Christian worship. In the preparation, therefore, of sacred song the most common expedient is to use the music of English and American churches. These tunes are composed for English verse. Only a few of these measures are found in Persian poetry. In some countries the custom, with missionaries, is to write the foreign words in English measure; but this cannot be done in Persian without such a departure from the rules of Persian versification as to shock the good taste of the intelligent and educated Persians. In the first hymns some were cast in the English measure to correspond with the music to which the words are set in English books, but in later translations it has been the purpose to follow the rules of Persian prosody.

In the autumn of 1875 and the following winter and spring there was a large attendance of Jews at the services of public worship on the mission-premises. As many as one hundred were sometimes present, also a goodly number of Armenians and some Mohammedans. The Jewish women were at all times the most disorderly persons in the congregation. In fact, all were quiet and respectful except them. They would talk aloud during the service with reference to all they saw and heard. The reproofs of their husbands and fathers were not sufficient to keep them in order. A result of the interest taken by the Jews was a request for a school in their colony. There was delay in acceding to the request, because that suitable buildings could not be had. There was now a school for Armenian children about half a mile from the Jewish quarter. Arrangements were made later to send the Jewish children to this school. The first week one hundred and twenty-five children attended. It was found to be necessary to limit the number. These children walked through the streets and bazars from the Jewish to the Armenian quarter. They were often set upon by Mohammedan children and Mussulmans and beaten. It was necessary to obtain the services of policemen to protect them as they went and came. Some months later the Armenian children were transferred to the school on the mission-premises and a house rented for the school in the Jewish quarter. The lack of funds caused the closing of the school in 1880, but it was re-opened in the following year under more favorable auspices, and was continued with good results. In 1883 an attempt was made by certain Jews to break up the school. The assistant teacher, a rabbi, was forced to leave the school with the children in his department. The principal of the school was a converted man and a member of the church at the time of this opposition. He appealed to the Persian authorities. His life had been threatened and the school-children were beaten from the door of the school. The parents of many of them were fearful, and the attendance was in this way greatly reduced. The authorities, however, finally caused the leaders of the opposition to be arrested and fined. The school was first opened with Mechail as superintendent; after him Caspar had control; but in 1881, and until 1884, the principal was a converted Jew named Baba, a physician of Tehran.

CHAPTER VII.

Organization of the Church in Tehran—Need of a Confession—Character of the Converts—Contributions—Hosein Ale, his Parents and Work—Preparation of Mohammedans for the Gospel—Relation of Officers of the Persian Government to Missionaries—The Sadr Azam—Colporteurs in Casveen—Summoned by the Governor—Their Work in the Villages—Hamadan—Changes of Preachers—Arrival of Kasha Shamoon—Sale of Books—Interest among Jews—Narrative of the Work among the Jews—Trials and Aims of the Jews—Firman for their Protection—Their Appeal to the British Society—Changes—Special Services—Publication of the Tract Primer—The Censor of the Press—Testimony of the Mujtaheed concerning the Primer—Other Translations—Mr. Potter's Tour to Mashhade Sar and Quarantine—Route to Mashhade Sar—Work of the New Missionaries—English Services—Statistics of 1878.

ONE of the most interesting events in the history of this mission was the organization of a church in Tehran on the 26th of March, 1876, with a membership of twelve native Persians. Of these, ten men and one woman were Armenians, and one man was a converted Mohammedan. Three elders and two deacons were chosen and ordained. The elders were Lazar, Mechail and Usta Abraham. The deacons were Caspar and Carepet. A short summary of doctrine and a covenant were adopted, and the same were subsequently used at the organization of the church in Hamadan. It is possible that a confession may not be necessary for every church, yet it would seem to be important on mission-fields, for many reasons. There is for the whole Church no common standard of belief, as in American and European churches, and in the present hostile attitude of the sects it would be difficult, if not impossible, to form one exactly in accord with the sentiments of one sect which would not be objectionable to another. That only would be satisfactory which is very general and elementary, comprehending the essentials of Christian doctrine. In the absence of such there is danger that the native preachers, each for himself, will undertake to form a creed for his church.

The Armenians, having been baptized in infancy, were not rebaptized; the Mohammedan convert was baptized. All these persons had been examined in their knowledge of Christian doctrine and duty and their evidences of piety. All professed a change of heart. After twelve years of acquaintance with them I know not that any one of them has denied the faith either by word or act. In succeeding years other persons have united with this church, and it gives promise of permanency and future influence. The members of the church began immediately to contribute of their income according to their ability. Contribution-boxes were put in the chapel by the side of each door; an account of the collections was kept by the deacons, and the annual report showed results creditable to the church. Several of the members were teachers, and others were pupils, in the mission-schools.

Of all these no one excited more interest than the convert from Islam. He was not the only one who was thought by the mission to be prepared for membership. He had been intimate with the native Christians and acquainted with the mission for nearly a year before making a public profession. His change of sentiments was, at the time, unknown to his family. Later, however, the fact became known to his mother, and then to his father, but they were anxious to conceal it. At first it was a source of great grief and alarm to his mother, who used every endeavor to change his purpose. Finally, when the report came to the father, he caused his son to be bound, and began to beat him, threatening to kill him; but his mother, hearing the noise, appeared on the scene and pleaded for her son. She was a first wife, and so entitled to more consideration than the other three wives. Her authority was recognized. The son, however, was not a favorite with his father, owing to the schemes of later wives, who wished to alienate the property. Hosein entered the service of the mission as a colporteur, and was very successful. He had two wives. To one of these, however, he was only betrothed, after the custom of the country. But that betrothal could not be broken any more readily than a marriage contract. It may seem not to be demanded by the Christian law that in such case he should be required to put either wife away if they were both minded to live with him after his change of religion. It is to be said, however, that Mohammedan marriage is not Christian marriage. The relation formed in it is from the first looked upon by both parties to the marriage as, possibly, a temporary one. The Mohammedan wife agrees to a divorce on payment of a stipulated sum. The divorce is not attended with any dishonor, but is taken to be a matter of course. The relation of husband and wife does not rest upon mutual affection, nor is it formed, at first, on any such ground. There are instances, no doubt, in which the divorce should not be insisted upon as a qualification for church-membership. The condition and necessities of the parties to be separated should be considered. From the first engagement of this man with the mission he has been a colporteur until now. He carried the Scriptures to the people on the plains of Ra and Varomene. He placed the Bible in several mosques in Tehran, where it was secretly studied by students of the schools. He carried books to Koom and Kashan on several occasions. In 1878 he was called to Mashhad to take charge of a depository in that city. He remained here during the year, laboring with marked success until his return to Tehran.

The inquiry may arise why Mohammedans in Persia are not affected by missionary labor? In answer it may be said that mission effort when directed to the two classes, Mohammedans and nominal Christians, finds them in very different conditions of mind. The former have no intellectual and religious preparation inclining them to accept the distinguishing doctrines of the gospel. Whatever of Christian truth has reached them has come in the distorted and perverted form presented in the Koran, and is intended to prejudice their minds against the Christian statement of the gospel. In every people which has been brought under the power of that gospel there has been a long period of preparation before any great reformation has been effected.

Officers of the Persian government seem to be very cautious not to identify themselves in any way with missions and missionaries. They are less cautious in the country than in the capital. Here association with the representatives of a foreign religion might be made use of by rivals, and any suspicion as to their religious proclivities would be equivalent to social ostracism. The men of rank have political and social standing which they guard with great caution, and to which they sacrifice every other interest. Men who are known as progressives among their own people furnish no exception to this statement. The late Sadr Azam had the reputation among Europeans and Persians of being a very liberal man, and of having used his influence for progress and the improvement of Persia. He cultivated friendly relations with foreign governments, and sought to introduce to Persia the education and arts of Europe. But as a reformer and progressive he was a great sham. His improvements did not extend beyond the adornment of the capital and the construction of a few telegraph-lines. In fact, he seems not to deserve the credit of the latter improvement. He interfered more with missionary work than the most bigoted Mohammedan who has held the office of minister of foreign affairs in late years. Every mission in Persia suffered restrictions during his administration; his appointees as sarparasts were most imbecile. He issued stringent orders concerning Mr. Bruce's work in Julfa; he put restrictions on converted Jews in Hamadan; and finally he issued, ostensibly by command of the Shah, those orders which made all foreign missionaries in that land a body of police to guard Mohammedans against Christian influences. When we consider that he was reputed to be more infidel than Mohammedan, and that his private life was understood to be licentious, his conduct with reference to missionaries can be reasonably accounted for only on the supposition that he was particularly desirous that no suspicion of sympathy with a foreign religion should rest upon himself.

At the close of the spring term of the school two young men were sent to the city of Casveen and the adjacent regions for the purpose of selling the Scriptures and other religious books. The city is wholly Mohammedan except a few Armenian inhabitants. Many of the people are Baubes, but secretly such, and outwardly are identified with the ruling sect. The colporteurs occupied a room in the caravansary, where in the course of a short time they were visited by many purchasers of books. Some of the mullahs complained to the governor of the work, and he ordered that Mohammedans should not purchase. This order, he claimed, was for the protection of the colporteurs. No doubt he expected to reap a double advantage, assuming to protect the booksellers and the interests of Islam. He ordered the young men to appear before him to investigate the reports. On the evening of June 19th two farashes were sent to conduct them to the governor's palace. They obeyed the summons, taking with them copies of the Scriptures. When asked what the doctrines of the Protestants were, they gave in reply a copy of the New Testament. The governor read portions of it, and pronounced it a good book. He said that he could not prohibit the sale of the books, because duty had been paid on them as articles of merchandise. He assured the colporteurs that he would protect them. They found, however, that the people had been so alarmed and that the mullahs were so opposed that their work was now at an end in this place; they therefore departed for Karaghan. One of them went on to Hamadan; the other spent the season in going to the Mohammedan villages between Karaghan and Sava. He openly offered the Bible for sale in the bazars and maidons of thirty-four villages, and sold a goodly number of books to the Mussulmans, yet met with no opposition.

A new impulse was now given to the work in Hamadan. I have stated that in consequence of the withdrawal of Deacon Guergues from that city Caspar had been sent thither. Guergues returned to Oroomiah in June, 1875, and in the following October, Caspar returned to Tehran to pursue his studies, and Priest Shamoon was sent from Oroomiah to take the place made vacant in Hamadan, and arrived in that city on the 6th of November. He preached in the Turkish language to the Armenians; he also gave attention to the sale of books. The bookstall in that city was now resupplied. Several boxes of the Scriptures in Hebrew were sold to the Jews. Books in Persian and Armenian were also in demand. The Protestants were now for the first time organized into a church. The first members were all Armenians, but in the course of the following two years much religious interest was excited among the Jews by the labors of the priest. This interest seemed to reach its height in the winter of 1877–78. Previous to this date no Jews were attendants on Christian worship. In 1877 some thirty Jews of Hamadan professed Christian sentiments, but they were not prepared for membership in the church, and many of them were moved to favor missionary effort among themselves from the expectation of political and secular advantage, hoping to receive protection against the extortion of Mohammedans. They wished the American mission to furnish them with schools. Many attended the preaching of Priest Shamoon. Meetings for religious worship were held in the houses of some of the people. The movement was met with the old spirit of intolerance, and persecution followed. The Jews of the synagogue sought the support of the Mohammedan authorities. The leaders of the Christian party were Doctors Jan and Raheem, and a jeweler named Hyim. Raheem was in favor with the authorities. The old party refused the Christian Jews entrance to the synagogues, baths and markets, on the pretext that, being Christians, they were unclean. The Christians sought to overcome opposition by an appeal to the Mohammedan authorities. At the solicitation of the Christian Jews, Mr. Bassett undertook to obtain an order from the Persian minister of foreign affairs for their protection. Such an order was issued. It declared the right of Jews to change their religious views and forms of worship and to become Christians or Armenians, and forbade any one to molest them in any way; but the same firman declared the right of the Jews to the undisturbed exercise of their religious rights—to own baths, shops and markets, and to admit or exclude therefrom whomsoever they would. This virtually sustained the right to exclude Christians. On this account the firman was not satisfactory to the reformers. They wished to compel the Jews to admit them to the baths and shops. A little later certain Armenians advised an appeal to Mr. Bruce and to the missionary societies of the Church of England, with a view to obtain the political or personal rights sought. Letters were written to the American missionary in Tehran having charge of the business saying that the old Jews must be forced to open their markets and shops to Christian Jews, and threatening a union with British societies unless such advantage could be obtained for them by the Americans. The missionary replied that no such orders could be reasonably expected or asked of the Persian government, and that the petitioners should be content with the liberty of their own convictions and personal rights. In 1878 a petition for schools and aid was drawn up by, or at the instigation of, an Armenian, signed by the greater part of the proselytes and forwarded to Mr. Bruce, and was then sent by him to the London Society for Promoting Christianity amongst the Jews. A favorable response was made by that society, and two years later two missionaries were sent by them to the Jews of Hamadan, but were withdrawn in 1884.

Mr. Potter left Tehran September 4, 1876, to attend the meeting of the Persian mission to be held in Oroomiah. He went to Tabriz, and thence to Oroomiah, in company with Mr. Easton. Mirza Mechail started for Rasht on the 20th of the same month to labor in that city. A few months later he was obliged to leave Rasht on account of the prevalence there of the plague. The week of prayer was observed by the church of Tehran in the first week of the year 1877, the members of the church and the missionaries conducting the exercises. In the spring of this year two of the training-class were sent to Hamadan and vicinity to labor as colporteurs.

The native teacher Ohanes returned to Shevarin, and one of the training-class was sent to take his place in the village of Tchenoktche in the mountains of Karaghan. Priest Megerditch was, at his own request, permitted to labor in the village and in the adjacent settlement. In Tehran special services for inquirers were held on Fridays, and the articles of the confession were at stated times explained to the members of the church and to all who thought of uniting with it.

The translation of the American Tract Society's Tract Primer having been completed by Mr. Bassett, that society made an appropriation for the publication of it. Some delay was occasioned by the effort to have the work printed in London, to secure better work, but it was found to be less expensive to publish it through a Mohammedan press in Tehran. The publication led to some interesting incidents showing the relation of the mission-work to the Persian authorities. It is required that every book printed shall be approved by the censor of the press before publication. His seal must be put upon the manuscript before the printer can put the work in the press. The seal of the censor was committed by him to his mother, as was also the prerogative of examining the manuscripts. When the manuscript of the Tract Primer was presented to her for her approval, she observed the illustrations and noted that the book was a Christian work, and ordered her scribe to examine it closely. The examination being completed, she said that she would not affix the seal to it, and that she had a mind to send both the book and the scribe who assisted in preparing it to the Shah. The scribe was a Persian mullah, and feared to do anything more in the matter. The printer, however, was more courageous and persistent. The subject was finally referred to the minister of science, who said that he would affix the seal provided any mujtaheed of Tehran would give his written approval of the publication. The manuscript having been taken to one of the mujtaheeds, he examined the work and discovered the expression "Jesus the Son of God." This he declared to be blasphemy and opposed to the teaching of Islam. Another judge of the religious law was more liberal, and wrote to the minister that as Mohammedans acknowledged Jesus to be a prophet, it would be lawful to print any book which honored him. On receiving this note and the usual fee, the seal was attached to the manuscript and the work was put into the hands of the printer. But these negotiations and examinations were protracted through the year, so that the work was not printed and bound until the spring of 1878.

In the spring of 1877, Mr. Potter began the translation of Bunyan's *Pilgrim's Progress*, Lazar began the preparation of a geography in Persian, and Mr. Bassett arranged to supervise a translation of the Gospel by Matthew into the Gaghattai Turkish. Information having been received that reinforcements for the mission would reach Persia in October, Mr. Potter volunteered to meet them at the Caspian port and escort them to Tehran. He left the capital on the 3d of October, going to Mashhade Sar, a port of the Persian Caspian coast. The plague had now nearly disappeared from Rasht, but there was no communication with the place, and passengers on steamers bound for Persia were obliged to land at other places. He remained in Mashhade Sar twelve days awaiting the party. The steamer having made a second trip, and no information having been received from them, he thought it best to go to Baku, thinking to meet the party there. He says: "We reached Mashhade Sar October 9th. On the 12th the steamer arrived, and it was ascertained from the captain that the boat did not run to Baku, but to Cape Apscheron, about three hours above Baku, and further that there was a strict quarantine at that point, a very unpleasant place to go through. As the captain very kindly offered his services to forward letters and messages to Baku, and to bring the party to Mashhade Sar, I concluded to take the captain's advice and send word to the party to come on to Mashhade Sar, and myself to remain at that point. After waiting twelve days the steamer again came around, and the captain not being able to get any information of the American party, I concluded to go to Apscheron, with the intention of trying to go through quarantine and proceed to Baku myself.

"Leaving Mashhade Sar October 24th, nine hours'

run brought us to Aschurada, and thence to Apscheron, where we arrived on the 27th, and I concluded to go into quarantine. My baggage was duly disinfected by a vapor of carbolic acid, and my money washed with some chemicals, and I took up my quarters in the summer tent with a dozen narrow bedsteads. The next day (October 28) the Astrakan steamer came in, bringing the expected party and releasing me from quarantine, to my inexpressible delight. I immediately re-embarked on the steamer, along with Mr. and Mrs. Scott and Miss Schenck, on our way to Tehran, where we arrived Friday night, November 9, 1877."

The route by Mashhade Sar crosses the highest regions of the Elburz Mountains and passes near the lofty peak of Damavand. The pass is in many places very precipitous, but is fairly passable by the roadway which in late years has been constructed by the order of the Shah. The borders of the Caspian are here, as at Rasht, a dense jungle and noted for malaria. In the summer and early autumn it is considered unsafe for Europeans to remain long in this region. Mr. Potter was taken ill with chills and fever on the return, and did not recover until after several months.

In the arrangements of the missionary work Miss Schenck was associated with Miss Bassett in the supervision of the girls' school, and Mr. Scott preached in English at the residence of Col. Smith, where for two winters the service of the Church of England had been read by some one of the English residents. The service was discontinued, as usual, in the spring, and Mr. Scott gave his attention to the study of the Persian.

About this time our religious services were attended by many Baubes. One of them was a very persistent caller, and brought to me several copies of the writings of the Baub of Akka. But in time he became very indignant that we did not accept the tenets of the sect, and charged that Christian teachers were as obstinate as Jews and Mohammedans, and contended that all who rejected the clear testimony furnished by the Baub ought to be put to death. There is in Tehran a representative or vakiel of the Baub. He looks after the interests of the sect in Persia, receives the communications of his superior in Syria and superintends the distribution of the messages and the preachers and the remittance of funds. This man called upon us at the mission-premises. He appeared to be a man of about sixty years of age. He is very corpulent and stout and is closely shaven. He was very desirous that we should listen to him, but his discourse was highly figurative and mystical. The principal points which he attempted to show were that the divine Person has always been manifested in the world since the creation. The manifestation was in the prophets, and later in Jesus Christ and Mohammed. The Baub, he claimed, is the last or latest revelation of Deity. A month later he called again, bringing his son-in-law, a resident of Savah. The vakiel's name is Hajah Mullah

Ismael. His visit was preceded by a servant bearing on a tray a present of rose-water, pomegranates and figs. The conversation of Ismael was of the same essential character as that of the previous visitor. It is indeed strange that these people should risk so much for so absurd a delusion. The Baub himself was once a resident of Tehran. His adherents have been moved with a zeal worthy of a better cause. The profession of the tenets of the sect is severely punished, in many cases with cruel torture and death.

CHAPTER VIII.

Departure of Mr. Potter for America—Departure of Mr. Bassett for Mashhad—Proposed Translation of the Gospel of Matthew—Colporteurs and Books for Mashhad—City and People—Fanatical Character of the Pilgrims and Mullahs—The Jews of Mashhad—Skeptics—Success of the Book-Agents Hosein and Daüd—Sequel of the Work in Mashhad—Book-Dépôt and Colportage—Mirza Daüd—His Work—Return to Tehran—Captive Georgians of Abasabad—Purchase of Premises in Tehran—Titles to Real Estate—Persecution of the Teacher in Karaghan—Supposed Secular Authority of Missionaries—Persecutions in Hamadan—Journey of Mr. Bassett to Hamadan—Visits Karaghan—The Armenian Settlement—Visit of Elders—Preaching—Desecration of the Sabbath—The Priest of Bargoshad—School—Journey by Night—A Village in Need—Appeal for the Sick—Arrival in Hamadan—Visit of the Jews—Their Wants—Jews Baptized—Audience with the Governor—Summer Work—Jews in Tajreesh—Marriage of the Rev. Mr. Potter—His Return to Persia—The Press—New Premises Occupied by the Girls' School—Sickness of Mrs. Scott—Return of Mr. Scott and Family to America—His Death and Character—Persecution of Jews in Hamadan—Orders of Persian Officers—Work in Tehran—Division of Bible-Work—Return of Mr. Bassett to the United States—Sickness by the Way—Work in London—Summary of the Work in Eastern Persia.

IN February, 1878, Mr. Potter left Tehran for the United States, going by post to Tabriz and Tiflis, thence by Pote and the continent.

Shrine of Reza.   Page 185.

Mr. Bassett had been authorized by the British and Foreign Bible Society to make a translation of Matthew's Gospel into the Takah dialect of the Turkmans, sometimes called the Gaghattai. He left Tehran in the month of April, going to Mashhad with a view to the introduction of the Scriptures there, and for the purpose of completing the arrangements made with the Bible Society for translating. Mechail and Carepet were to accompany him as colporteurs. Several boxes of books were sent on by caravan with these men as far as to Shah Rud. The missionary followed later by chapar, overtaking the colporteurs and caravan, according to appointment, at that place. All caravans were escorted from this point, a distance of four days' travel, by a company of soldiers, this part of the route having long been considered unsafe, owing to the raids of the Turkmans. A lengthy account of this journey has been given in another volume, and need not be repeated here.

No place in Persia is so sacred to the Sheah as Mashhad, for here is the grave of the only Imam buried in that kingdom. It has been called the "holy," in honor of the eighth Imam, who was interred here. There is at all times a large number of pilgrims in the city from every Mohammedan country in Asia. It might be thought that so noted a place would exhibit the highest type of Oriental architecture, but, the shrine of Reza excepted, there is nothing noteworthy in the city. The streets are narrow, crooked and filthy, the central avenue alone excepted. Whatever attempt has been made in the way of building and decoration appears to have been exhausted on the shrine of Reza; but of this nothing is visible to the traveler entering the city or to one without the walls of the shrine, except the gold-tiled dome and lofty minarets. The broad avenue leading to the mosques called Reza is crowded with markets and a motley throng of rough and fierce-looking people, in which the dervishes are most conspicuous. As many of this throng of pilgrims as desire it are fed from the bounty of the shrine. The six hundred pounds of rice furnished daily by the mosque would seem to be a small allowance for the crowd, the guards and priests.

This did not seem to be the safest place for missionary work, but there could be no question as to the need of the people and the certainty of an audience. The mullahs were said to be a dangerous set of fellows. The crowd that filled the streets was to all appearance equally desperate and fanatical. Adoration of Reza was the popular act, whatever the secret sentiments of the people may have been. The dervishes were many and of all orders, but the wandering and beggarly element seemed to predominate. Yet neither the missionary nor the colporteurs were molested. The colporteurs entered the city several days after the arrival of the missionary, and paid duty on their books at the custom-house in Scriptures. In a few days they sold all the books they had

Dervish. Page 189.

brought with them, and they received orders from Jews for two more loads. These were immediately ordered from Tehran. But the colporteurs desired to leave the city with the missionary, for they feared to remain after his departure and dared not leave the place alone. He therefore accompanied them a day's journey, and put them in charge of a caravan bound for Tehran. The people who resorted to the colporteurs most of all were Jews, for there were no Armenians or Christians in the city. It has been reported that the mullahs have vowed that no Armenians or other non-Mohammedans shall reside in the place; for they say, " It would be a dishonor to our shrine and holy city to permit any 'infidels' to live within the sacred precincts." They seem to have acted on this principle many years ago, when [*] they raided the Jewish quarter, killing some thirty-five Jews and giving the balance of the colony the alternative of the Koran or death. The Jews were the principal purchasers of both Hebrew and Persian Scriptures. Many of the books were bought for the use of the Jews of this city, and many to be carried to Herat and settlements of Jews in Turkistan. The condition of this remnant of Israel is sad to contemplate. They have been forced to deny the religion of their fathers. The worship of God after the law of Israel is observed in secret if at all. Some of this people manifested intense interest in religious matters, and came for inquiry and

[*] 1838.

discussion. It was evident that even in this remote quarter of the world some of this people were not lacking in current objections to the Scriptures. Two Jews desired to meet the missionary for the purpose of considering the Messiahship of Jesus. One of the first questions proposed was how the genealogical tables given by Matthew and Luke could be reconciled. The Jews, however, were not the only parties who manifested deep interest in the work of the missionary and seemed to give encouragement for effort in this city. Some of the Mohammedans were apparently dissatisfied with the prevalent faith and forms of worship. Here were the extremes of fanaticism and unbelief. One man, whose name and place should be suppressed for his protection, who had been to Constantinople and had made the pilgrimage to Makkah, and seen all of Islam, yet said, "I do not keep the fast, and I am not afraid of being defiled by Christians, but I must pretend to be a good Mohammedan, which I am not, for the sake of my wife, who is the daughter of a sayed." Another of high rank said, "The people of this city are not sincere Mohammedans; many are disgusted with the shams and tricks perpetrated by the mullahs of Persia." Such were the openings for Christian labor here that Hosein Ale of Tehran was ordered from that city to remain in Mashhad during the year. He wrote a few weeks after his arrival that he could do much more in the way of selling books here than he could do in the capital. He ordered a good supply of the Scriptures, which was forwarded to him in due time.

A Jew of Mashhad by the name of Daüd was here employed by Mr. Bassett to assist in the work of the proposed translation. His boyhood and youth had been spent among the Turkmans of Ahäl and Merv. In later years he had lived among the tribes as doctor and merchant. He remained in Tehran several months, and on completion of the translation returned to Mashhad. On the return of Hosein to the capital Daüd was employed as a colporteur, and later as a book-agent, in which capacity he has served until the present time, having charge of the book-supply for Mashhad.

The proposed translation was completed in 1879, and printed in 1880 by the British and Foreign Bible Society, and a supply of the books was sent to Mashhad. These with other Scriptures in Turkish, Persian and Hebrew have been sent to the country of the Turkmans and to Herat, and to the people on the eastern border of Persia.

The missionary returned to Tehran over the route by which he had come, reaching that city on the 29th of May. In the account of this journey special mention is made of the colony of Georgians living in Abasabad. Being Christians by their antecedents and at heart, they naturally excite the sympathies of other Christians. Like the Jews of Mashhad, they have been compelled in the course of time to profess Islam. Their condition, both religious and secular, seems to be all the more deplorable when we consider from what they have fallen and what they have suffered. The priest of the colony, though ostensibly a mullah, desired that efforts should be made in behalf of his people. But labors for their good must be of a radical nature. There seems to be no hope of permanent benefit to them except in their removal, for they are helpless in the midst of Mohammedans, and are isolated from all the Christian colonies.

During the summer negotiations were entered into for the purchase of premises for the mission in Tehran. The purchase seemed to be necessary for many reasons. Persian houses require a continual expenditure of funds in the way of repairs, and little hope can be entertained that the owner of the property will ever make these repairs according to agreement. He is usually in great need of funds, and nothing can be done with him without payment of a large part of the rental in advance. Having obtained this, he is quite sure that his tenant will make the repairs rather than see the roof fall in or leave the premises and lose the advance payment. In the growth of the city there was a demand for houses, and the price of real estate was rapidly advancing. The best locations and best opportunities for the purchase of property were lost in those early days for the lack of the necessary funds. Some small purchases were made for a chapel and schools, but these were not at any time thought to be or designed to be the permanent locations to be occupied by the mission families. It had been the wish of the mission to purchase land near the Casveen gate, so as to be near the Armenian colony in that quarter, but the lack of funds and the unsettled state of the title to vacant lands in that vicinity made such purchase impossible or inexpedient. Purchase here being impracticable, the opportunities presented in the northern part of the city should have been seized, but these occurred during the years of the greatest financial embarrassment of the Board in New York, and could not, therefore, be taken advantage of. The property now bought was situated in the district known as the Shimron gate, and on the western side of the king's garden, Lala Zar, and the roofs of the houses commanded a view of the garden. The property was owned by a European officer of the king's army; the buildings were erected for his own use. One inducement to this purchase was the promise of a recognition of the transfer by the Persian Foreign Office, which would be an important concession to the mission. It was felt that the premises were not all that were needed, but they were well located, gave room for present needs and were ready for immediate occupancy, saving the loss of time required to build. But, more than all, they were as extensive as the funds of the mission would permit them to purchase. The buildings ready for occupancy were three, and furnished accommodations for the girls' school and two families. They readily rented for three hundred tomans, or six hundred dollars, which was twelve per cent. on the price paid to purchase them. On examination it was found that it would require some action by the authorities to perfect the title. The completion of these formalities was not effected until the autumn. The deeds were finally recognized by a mujtaheed and sealed at the Foreign Office. A person unaccustomed to the transfer of property in Persia can hardly realize the difficulties which attend such transfer. The possession of all the deeds from the first sale is thought to be necessary as evidence of title. A registry of conveyances should be kept by every mujtaheed who takes the acknowledgments, but the greater part of these papers are never put on record. The land now purchased comprised about four thousand seven hundred square yards. Of the three houses on it, one was well adapted to the wants of the girls' school.

During the summer the teacher in the Armenian village of Tchenoktche, Karaghan, met with bitter opposition from Mussulmans. A lawsuit had been begun by a Mohammedan claimant of the village against the Armenian owner. The teacher, being an Armenian and having entered the village under the auspices of the Armenian owner, became an object of enmity to the new claimant. It is probable that the opposition was instigated and encouraged by some of the Armenians of the neighboring villages. Orders were obtained from the minister of foreign affairs requiring redress of the wrongs done to the young man and that he should be protected; but the order was entirely disregarded by the Mohammedan landlord. A party of six horsemen rode into the village, seized the teacher and forced him to go with them to another village. He escaped at night and fled to the governor of the district, who protected him and procured for him a safe return to his school. This young man was Ohanes, now for several years connected with the mission in Hamadan.

The missionary in Persia is frequently constrained to intercede with the authorities for the protection of the native Christians. Owing to the influence of the foreign legations, the power of the missionary in secular matters is very greatly overrated by the natives, and any refusal by him to give assistance is taken by them as evidence of ill-will on his part or of disinclination to help them out of their troubles, which often arise because they are Christians or at least are favorably disposed toward missionaries.

A Mohammedan once came to the missionary in Tehran bringing a decree of an eminent mujtaheed of Ispahan setting over to him certain lands near that city. The decree had been resisted by the authorities of Ispahan. The man desired the missionary to command H. B. M. minister to issue an order for the restoration of the property agreeably to the judgment of the mujtaheed. The man argued thus: The missionary is a Christian mujtaheed; he has the same authority with his own people that a mujtaheed of Islam has with Mohammedans, and the decree of the mujtaheed is sufficient evidence of the equities of the case.

With the first movement of the Jews of Hamadan toward Christianity, whether from true or improper motives, there appeared also the spirit of persecution. The Mohammedan authorities and their subordinates were used as the tools of the opposition. They gladly favored one party or another as they perceived the opportunity to extort money from them. In this state of affairs it seemed to be important that the missionary in charge of the work in Hamadan should go to that city, agreeably to the request of the pastor of the native church and of the people. Mr. Bassett therefore left Tehran for that city on the 24th of October, going by post. After reaching Bevaron, a post-station on the pass of the Karaghan Mountains, and nearly midway between Tehran and Hamadan, he crossed the mountains to the northern side and to the Armenian settlement comprising the villages of Lar, Bargashod, Tchenoktche, Yange Kallah and Zambar. In the first are sixty families; in the second, forty; in the third, fifty; in the fourth, twenty-five; and in the fifth, fifteen. They are near together, no one of them being more than four miles from Lar. Together they may contain a population of one thousand Armenians, besides Mussulmans. These people refer the origin of their colony to the captives brought by Shah Abas to Ispahan, and in particular to the portion of the captive colony brought from Utch Kallesia. But they have received accessions from other places. The first company started from Julfa near Ispahan, and led for several years a roving life, settling at Savah, Tehran, Kazas and Kamara. They say that pure air, arable land and a copious spring of water at Bargashod, furnishing water sufficient for the tillage of five villages, were the chief attractions. Several years ago a large part of the colony went to the Karadag in Russia, but, becoming dissatisfied, they returned to Karaghan. These villages are all in a deplorable state of ruin. In three of them there are churches, but part of the walls and roofs had fallen, so that they could not be occupied.

The further account of this settlement and this visit of the missionary may best be given, for the most part, in the words of his report. He wrote: "Our schoolteachers had been sent to the village of Tchenoktche. I therefore went immediately to that place. On Sabbath morning the elders made a formal call. The time was spent in religious conversation. They professed to accept our statement of Christian doctrine. They urged their need of schools and preachers, but fear of the priest and of the suspicion of Protestant tendencies prevented any very decisive recognition on their part. They evidently desired schools, but not a religious service, and made no effort to gather the people for public worship on the Sabbath. The men went off to the fields to work or to visit in other villages. Near sunset squads of men and droves of donkeys were seen coming down the mountain. I determined to raise a congregation, and therefore, calling the people nearest to me, I went on to the little hill in the centre of the village, where there was an open space and a spring of water, and calling also the people who were coming into town, I soon had a congregation such as the village could afford. The company of tax-gatherers who at that time came along the way gave variety to the costume of the crowd by the red and white shawls tied around their heads and by the knives and pistols stuck in their girdles. On Monday morning I went up to Bargashod, three miles distant. The only Armenian priest of the settlement resides here. He appeared to be very friendly, and it was arranged that he should open a school in his house; but later he wrote that some of the members of his flock had charged him with having sold the people to the Protestants, and demanding, as a condition on which alone the arrangements could be carried into effect, that he should divide his bribe with them. As, however, he had received nothing, a division was not possible. After having gone to each village in succession and preached to as many people as could be gotten together, I started on my return to the post-road, said to be about four farasangs distant, intending to reach that day the post-house at Nobaron. Going southward from Lar, I passed the village of Zambar. The villagers had seen our colporteurs in former years. Crossing the Karaghan range, it was dusk before we reached the foot of the mountain. In a short time it was dark and raining. Our chapar shagird lost his way. We rode until eleven o'clock at night, when the barking of a dog enabled us to find a village. One of the horses fell into a ditch, throwing his rider, whose foot was fast in the stirrup. Dismounting, I held the horse while the man extricated himself. Arriving at the village gate, we were obliged to give an account of ourselves before the people would open for us. Our men made all necessary explanations. It was therefore soon known that a 'Frangee' was near. Men and women gathered about us, and much was said by them of which we caught a few expressions, such as these: Good men these are! the best kind of a millat (sect).—They have all kinds of asbob (machinery).—I want some medicine.—They have the best doctors.—Are you a doctor? A special plea was made in behalf of a very sick person who was said to be dying. His poor wife insisted that I must be a doctor, my statement to the contrary notwithstanding, and that I could cure him even if I were not a doctor. Leaving the company at the gate, I went with one of our men to the hut of the sick man. Here I found a Mussulman doctor wanting antimony. Several children were lying near a kursee, and the sick man lay close by them. The matron of the hut, greatly concerned for her husband, disclosed the wretchedness of the situation by the light of a rag soaking in an open earthen oil-lamp which she held in her hand. Doing all that I could for the sick man, who did not seem to be so ill as represented, I departed, followed by the blessings of the wretched people. Taking a guide at this village, after an hour's ride we arrived at the post-house in Nobaron." On the following morning the missionary resumed the journey to Hamadan.

Arriving in that city, the missionary visited the Jewish quarter, and many Jews called upon him. A large number of the people seemed inclined to Christianity, but only a few had taken any positive stand in relation to it. Some thirty Jews called upon the missionary for consultation with reference to the establishment of a mission among them. The matter was fully discussed. They were told that a school would be opened for them in the Jewish quarter as soon as possible. In the mean time, the priest Shamoon was instructed to preach among them, which he was himself forward to do. But it was impossible to give any assurance that missionaries would be sent from America expressly for them. The matter of their appeal to the British society was openly discussed, and they were told that the American mission would not attempt to compete with any other society or appear as a rival. They replied that the petition had been sent when they supposed that we could not help them. They were advised to attend the religious services held in the Armenian church, but conducted in the Persian language, which they well understood. Three

Jews were at this time examined by the elders of the church and the missionary, and were publicly baptized and received by him to the communion in the church. In the examination they all attributed their religious interest to the labors of Shamoon. Two of these men, Dr. Raheem and Hyim, were persons of intelligence and influence. The governor of the city at this time was the Eelkhanah. On one occasion the missionary was given audience to present the grievances of the Jews, and he was invited to dine with the governor, at which time that officer promised to protect the converts and to redress any wrong done them. But it was a difficult matter to separate present complaints from old feuds, and as yet there had been no violence offered a convert on account of his religious convictions. Six Jews had been received to the communion before the close of 1879.

During the summer months the mission remained in the village of Tajreesh. Mr. Bassett was engaged in the translation work with Mirza Daüd of Mashhad. Services of public worship were here conducted in Persian, and were attended by the Mohammedans and Armenians. The latter were from the villages of Darooz and Vanak. Although not permitted to attend Protestant services while the missionaries officiated in or near an Armenian village, they now came several miles to the service, and escaped the observation of the priest and avoided all molestation. A few Jews from the city of Tehran came to Tajreesh and attended the religious services at the mission, but they feared the Mohammedans and sought protection in the neighborhood of the mission. During the time of worship a Mohammedan would quietly pull a Jew from a bench or chair and take the seat himself. For so long a time have the Jews been accustomed to such treatment that they seldom remonstrate.

Mr. Potter married Miss Harriet Riggs at her home in New Jersey on the 1st of August, 1878, and with his bride returned to Tehran in the following November, arriving in that city on the 14th of that month. An appropriation for the purchase of a printing-press and type had been made by the annual meeting of the mission in the autumn of 1874. The press was now bought by Mr. Potter, and with the press the necessary outfit for printing by the lithographic process. Owing, however, to the pressure of other work and lack of suitable building, the press has not been used. Printing has been done at the Mohammedan presses in Tehran as far as work has been needed.

Before the arrival of Mr. Potter the mission returned to the city from Tajreesh, and entered for the first time the premises purchased this season as above stated. The girls' school was removed to the building set apart for it. Mr. Scott and family occupied this building with the ladies in charge of the school. The instruction was in the Armenian tongue, but some of the older scholars

Mission Premises, Tehran.

Page 205.

studied the Persian. Religious services were conducted by Miss Bassett in the Armenian language. There was no room or house on the mission-premises suitable for a chapel. A large stable was therefore overhauled and plastered, and made a very tidy and fair room. In this the congregation of Persians assembled on Fridays and Sabbaths until the autumn of 1883 and the completion of a larger chapel.

The health of Mrs. Scott was such at this time that it was thought to be advisable by the physicians consulted that she should return to America. Mr. Scott therefore left Tehran on the 27th of November. He remained some weeks in Scotland and England. The physicians consulted there advised quiet and rest. This could not be had among strangers, and the party therefore hastened home, and arrived in New York in the following March, where, after a brief illness, Mr. Scott died within a week after his arrival. Mr. Scott when he came to Persia was reported to be a person of unusually good health. His robust frame seemed to justify his statement that he had never experienced any serious illness. He was a graduate of Princeton College and Seminary, and had the reputation of being a good classical scholar. His first and only year in Persia was devoted chiefly to the study of the Persian language. He rendered good service by preaching in English and by performing some secular work. He did not remain on the field long enough to preach in the Persian language. His death was felt to be a great loss to the mission, for much had been anticipated from his promising abilities.

Early in the winter of 1879 great excitement was created among the Jews of Hamadan by special efforts on the part of the Jews of the synagogues to prevent Christian Jews from entering the synagogues and baths owned by Jews. The governor called Eelkhanah had been recalled, and a new governor appointed who favored the old party. The orders of the Jewish priests forbidding the sale of food and merchandise to the converts was confirmed by the order of the Persian minister, on the ground that the converts could purchase in other places or have their own shops, and that, as they could have their own places of worship, they should not trespass upon the right of other Jews to the exercise of their own religious laws. In the absence of the minister recourse was had to the Mustofe al Mamalake, who issued an order to restrain the persons opposing the converts, and requiring that Christians should be protected and permitted to enter the synagogue; but the order was disregarded by the local authorities. In this year there was opened a school for Jews in Tehran, as has been stated. A thousand volumes of the new edition of the Scriptures in small size were now received from the British and Foreign Bible Society by way of the Persian Gulf, and colporteurs were immediately sent out with the books. In this year arrangements were discussed for the division of the Bible-work in Persia between the two Bible societies, the British and Foreign and the American Bible Society. It was proposed that the former should supply the southern half of the country, and the latter the northern part. Such an arrangement was carried into effect in the following year. Teachers were again sent to the Armenians of the Karaghan Mountains, the translation of the Gospel of Matthew into the dialect of the Takah Turkmans was completed, and Mirza Daüd returned to Mashhad.

On the 20th of August, 1879, Mr. Bassett and family left Tehran for America, having been in Persia for eight years. One of the children was very ill, and, owing to the heat of the day, the party were obliged to travel by night over the plain of Tehran and to the pass of the Elburz. The post-road to Casveen was not yet completed, and the journey was made by caravan. Remaining in Casveen over the Sabbath, they left early on Sunday evening to journey by night, but, the sick child becoming much worse, they were obliged to halt and return to Casveen. Being ninety-two miles from Tehran, it was impossible to get the aid of a European physician. In this emergency a Mohammedan doctor was called. Although it was now the time of the long fast of Ramazan, and he declined to respond to the call of native Persians, yet he immediately went at night to see the child of the missionary, and his treatment was so efficient that in two days the party were able to journey, being supplied with a good stock of medicines prepared by the doctor.

The little patient gradually recovered, but was not entirely well until the party experienced the effect of the cold climate of Europe. Mr. Bassett remained in London during the autumn and part of the winter of 1880, superintending the publication of the Takah translation. In February the party crossed the Atlantic to the United States, where they remained until April, 1881.

In the year 1879 there were in Tehran, connected with the mission, two regular congregations, two places of worship and three schools. There were thirty church-members and one hundred and thirty pupils in the schools of the city. The church in Hamadan numbered thirty-two members and about sixty attendants, with a school of thirty pupils. Schools were established in Rasht and Karaghan and in the village of Darooz, and the work of Bible-distribution was carrried on upon the eastern border of Persia from Mashhad, and in much of Central Persia from Tehran and Hamadan, as part of the regular work of the mission.

CHAPTER IX.

Schools—Marriages—Persecutions in Hamadan—Represented to the British Minister—Yasse Attar—Position of the British Minister—Reasons for—Orders of the Shah touching the Attendance of Mohammedans at the Religious Services and the Instruction of Mohammedans—Attendance Prohibited by the Missionary—Liberty of Non-Mohammedans—Protestant Village—Expediency of forming Christian Villages—Mr. Bruce in Hamadan—Arrival of Mr. Hawkes in Tehran—Bookroom opened in Hamadan—Death of Agah Jan—Mussulmans Received to the Church—Proposed Occupation of Hamadan—Visit of Missionaries and Mr. Whipple to Hamadan—Work in Hamadan—Division of the Bible-Work in Persia—Report of the year 1880—Girls' School—Persecutions in Hamadan—Persecution of the Pastor—Return of Mr. Bassett and Family—Dr. W. W. Torrence—Voyage on the Caspian—Detention at Ashurada—Journey to Tehran—Changes in the Persian Foreign Office—Flight of Shamoon to Tehran—His Return to Hamadan—Meeting of the Persian Mission—Division of the Mission—Appointment of Mr. Hawkes to Hamadan—Consideration of the Orders of the Persian Government—Copy of the Action taken by the Mission sent to the British Minister—Reply of the Minister—Attendance of Mohammedans—Efforts for a Modification of the Orders—Refusal of the British Minister to Interfere for a Modification—Mission Resolve to Close the Chapel—Appeal to the Persian Foreign Office and to the Shah—Modification granted by the Shah—The Chapel Opened—Two Missions in Hamadan—Mr. Potter Removes to the Western Side of the City—Dr. Torrence opens a Dispensary—Mirza Lazar goes to Rasht—English Services—School for Jews—Nurillah—Boarding-School—Services of Worship and Schools—

Miss Bassett Returns to America—Protestant Chapel and Cemetery—Eclipse of the Sun.

IN January, 1880, the school for Jews in Tehran was closed for lack of funds. The training-class was dismissed. Four of the members of this class married, and were employed as teachers or colporteurs. Caspar and Carepet married daughters of Mechail. The young ladies had for some years been members of the girls' school, and for more than a year had been betrothed to these young men, in accord with the Armenian custom.

New cases of persecution arose in Hamadan, and Mr. Potter represented them to the British minister, who directed the British agent in that city to inquire into them, and, if possible, get the offenders punished. But he declined to give the agent any general directions as to the protection of Jewish converts. In the month of March a telegram from Hamadan announced that the Jew Yasse Attar had been severely beaten and thrown into prison, and that nothing had been done for him or for other Jews by the British agent. The telegram was referred to the British minister, who replied that he could not interfere officially, but would speak to the Sapr Salar about it. No promise or hope of redress was offered at the British legation. It should be said, in reference to the position taken by the minister on this subject, that the representatives of foreign governments do not claim to have any right to interfere *officially* in behalf of the subjects of the Persian government. They can act in such cases only unofficially, on the grounds of personal friendship or other reason. However, *unofficial* action is usually sufficient to furnish the Persian authorities with all the cause or apology which they need for granting the request of a representative of a foreign court. The force of any appeal by a foreign minister depends very much upon the relations of his government to the Shah and upon his own standing with the Persian authorities.

On April 2d a note was addressed to Mr. Potter by the British minister which stated, in substance, that it had been brought to the notice of the Shah that of late religious meetings held on the mission-premises had been attended by Mohammedans, and that he had received official communication on the subject setting forth the objections of the Shah's government to religious instruction being given to Mussulmans. He also added that "should he continue in the course complained of, the Persian government would not allow him to reside here;" also adding that the police had received orders to arrest any Mussulmans who may attend the meetings. On the same day the missionary replied to the communication that he had issued orders directing that no Mussulmans be allowed to attend the religious services or schools. As a compensation for this restriction touching Mohammedans the British minister said that he had obtained orders with reference to the Jews and the religious liberty of non-Mohammedans. On the 16th of November following the minister obtained, or communicated, an order from the Persian minister addressed to the governor of Hamadan, directing that the Jews who have become Christians be allowed to go to the bath-house "which is open to Armenians and Nestorians," and in December an order was issued by the same Persian officer to the governor of Hamadan declaring expressly the religious liberty of all non-Mohammedans in Persia.

An effort was now made to concentrate the Protestant Armenians in one village called Zard Aub. With reference to this Mr. Potter wrote in the report of that year as follows: "A new out-station has been opened about twenty-five miles from Tehran, and an attempt made to establish a Protestant village under the auspices of the elders of the Tehran church. A tentative occupation was begun in the spring, and it is hoped this place will prove a refuge for Christian converts where they may enjoy the quiet exercise of their religion and be secure in their rights as tenants." But these expectations were disappointed by reason of the unhealthfulness of the location, and after much sickness and several deaths the village in the following year was abandoned. With reference to the expediency of isolating Christian converts in villages exclusively their own and enjoying special secular advantages, the author of this work would here express no judgment, but he would give to his readers, especially the missionaries, the benefit of the statement that the expediency has been questioned by missionaries of long experience; and there are examples of such villages in Persia and other Mohammedan countries where the results have been disastrous rather than beneficial to the people gathered in them. The question, however, would seem to be one which must be determined by the circumstances in which the people are placed, rather than by any general rule. It would seem to be safe, however, to say that under a government habitually and notoriously false to its own pledges the less the missionary has to do with the secular affairs, especially the rights of property of the people, the better it will be for his influence with all classes, and so much the less of his time will be lost.

Mr. Bruce, of the Church Missionary's mission in Julfa, visited the city of Hamadan in the month of November, and heard representations of the Jews of that place. In the report of the London Society for Promoting Christianity amongst the Jews it is stated, in substance, that the representations of Mr. Bruce encouraged that society to project a mission to Hamadan expressly for the Jews of that city.

On the 4th of December, 1880, Rev. J. W. Hawkes arrived in Tehran, having been appointed to the mission in the capital by the "Board" in New York. Mirza Ohanes was sent to open a bookroom in Hamadan, the room having been dispensed with now for several years, owing to the little amount of work done in the book-business there. Agah Jan, one of the leaders of the

Jewish converts, died in November of this year, leaving his family in very destitute circumstances, and aid was given them. The mission in Tehran resolved that Mussulmans, applicants for church-membership, should be examined, and if their examination proved satisfactory they should be received into the Church. Soon after this two Mussulmans were examined as to the evidences of their faith in Christ, and one of the number was received to the communion. Proposals were made in Tabriz looking to the occupation of Hamadan by some of the missionaries of the former city, but action in the matter was deferred. The members of the mission in Tehran, in company with Mr. Whipple, then agent of the American Bible Society in Persia, went to Hamadan. They record their great satisfaction in view of the work in that city and their reception by the people. They agreed to the opening of a school among the Jews, and engaged Hyim as teacher and evangelist, and made arrangements for the purchase of land for a chapel and cemetery. The congregation at the time was stated to consist of "forty men, thirty women and twenty children—in all ninety souls."

The American Bible Society now assumed the support of the colporteur at Mashhad and part of the expenses of the agents in Tehran and Hamadan. Mr. Bruce now came to Tehran in the interest of the British and Foreign Bible Society, making a division and sale of the books of that society in Tehran; and having completed these arrangements, he returned to Ispahan. Thus the two Bible societies were fully installed in Persia, each one having a general agent—one, Mr. Whipple, residing in Tabriz, and the other, Mr. Bruce, resident in Julfa (Ispahan). These facts have value as showing the growth and prosperity of Bible-work in Persia.

The report for the year 1880, as made by Mr. Potter, presents the progress of the mission in the following statements: "Only two members have been received to the church in Tehran the past year, making the present membership on the roll thirty-one. Contributions exclusive of the subscription of missionaries have amounted to $95, of which the sum of $54 was expended in part support of a native helper at Tehran, and $10 was sent to Oroomiah for the relief of the famine-sufferers." With reference to Hamadan he writes: "The Nestorian pastor has continued his services with acceptance. Four have been received into the church, and one has died, leaving the number of members thirty-five. The contributions have amounted to $88, of which $45 was for famine relief at Oroomiah, and $22 toward the support of the native pastor. The Jewish movement at Hamadan seems to be growing in importance, demanding some forward movement on the part of the mission. Repeated efforts for the protection of the persecuted converts seem at length to have been crowned with complete success. An order from the Persian minister of foreign affairs to the governor of Hamadan has at length brought peace to the oppressed. The leader in this awakening among the Jews has been called to his reward.

"Work in the Karaghan district was given up in the summer, because of a very disturbed state of affairs resulting from the disputed ownership of the village, which caused many of the Armenians to desert the place in fear.

"Interest in the Scriptures has increased, and our sacred book has been placed in the hands of a number of Persians of high rank who expressed a desire to examine it. Sales during the year, 430 volumes, amounting to $117. A stock of the Turkish Matthew, translated by Mr. Bassett, has been received from the British and Foreign Bible Society, and a supply sent to Mashhad, from whence some have been forwarded to Merv, Bokhara and to two other points in the interior of Turkistan.

"The girls' boarding-school of Tehran has had a prosperous year, reaching the full number of twenty pupils. Owing to the high prices which have prevailed, and which still continue, it has been a very difficult problem to carry on the school with the amount allowed in the estimate.

"It seems impossible to sustain a good boys' school at Tehran without a large expenditure for instruction, more especially as it has not been practicable for the missionaries to teach in the school for several years. At present one teacher is engaged, having twelve pupils. The school at Hamadan, including both boys and girls, reports thirty-one in attendance. We regret to say that the divisions and a want of brotherly feeling among the members of this church [in Tehran] became painfully apparent early in the year, which have excited a chilling influence."

In the course of the summer of 1881 additional rooms were constructed for the girls' school, and two rooms were added to the chapel on the west side, to be used for manual labor, where the boys of the school might learn shoemaking and tailoring.

In the month of September word was sent by telegraph to Mr. Potter from the pastor in Hamadan of fresh persecutions in that city. Mr. Potter again referred the matter to the British minister, who promised to see the Persian minister on the subject. The cases of persecution were these: Two Jewish converts were seized, beaten and imprisoned, and were released on a condition of the payment of a fine of seventy-five tomans. An attempt was also made to collect again a tax of fifty tomans additional, about half the amount remitted by express firman of the Shah some six years previous to this time. Pastor Shamoon had been very active and bold in his efforts with the authorities in behalf of the Jews and Armenians. He sent the telegram. On this account the governor caused him to be arrested and bound to be flogged, but by the intercession of Dr. Raheem he was released, but with threats for the future should he meddle with the affairs of these people. Greatly exasperated and mortified, and fearing lest the threats made might be put in execution, the pastor fled to the protection of Zain al Abadeen at Shevarin. The members of the church in Hamadan sent a petition to the missionary in Tehran asking redress for the insult and violence offered the priest, and desiring relief from the taxes. These papers were referred to the British minister that he might present them to the Persian minister.

Mr. Bassett and family left the United States on their return to Persia in May, 1881. They remained in London until the 25th of August. While in that city he reviewed, by request of the committee of publication of the British and Foreign Bible Society, a part of the manuscript of Mr. Bruce's revision of the New Testament in Persian, with a view to the expediency of its publication. He also called upon the secretaries of the London Society for Promoting Christianity amongst the Jews, acquainting them with the work carried on by the American mission in Hamadan.

Dr. W. W. Torrence, a graduate of Rush Medical College of Chicago, had been appointed medical missionary for Tehran, and he had arranged to join the party with Mr. Bassett for the journey to Persia. Arriving with his wife in London as arranged, the party left that city at the time above stated, and traveled by way of Berlin, Czaritzin and Astrakhan, thence by steamer on the Caspian. Storms prevailed on that sea, so that they were unable to effect a landing at Anzile, the steamer running directly across from Lankoran to Ashurada. Here they were obliged to land, and wait until the steamer coming from the north on the eastern side of the Caspian should arrive, that it might take them back to Anzile. Ashurada is the name given to a natural bay and harbor at the south-eastern extremity of the Caspian. The harbor is commodious, but there is no settlement here, on the Persian shore, of any importance. The only village, Gaz, is a small cluster of thatched and filthy huts. The country adjacent is a dense jungle in which tigers, leopards and other wild animals abound, but the mosquitoes are more formidable than the tigers, and the malaria is more to be feared than all the wild animals, the mosquitoes included. This is such that it is unsafe for foreigners and the unacclimated to tarry here at all. Fortunately, the party were obliged to remain but a night, as the steamer bound westward came on the following day and took them to Anzile, where they were able to effect a landing, for there was now here a calm sea, so that boats could pass the roadstead.

The party remained in Rasht two days to make arrangements for the journey by land. While here the Armenians renewed their request for missionaries and schools. The party now crossed the Elburz to Casveen, going by night over the Hazon pass. At Casveen they met Mr. Wilson and Miss Jewett of the mission in Tabriz on their way to the annual meeting of the Persian mission to be held in Tehran. Both were now ill of chills and fever. As post-wagons could be obtained at this place, the remainder of the journey was made with rapidity. Miss Jewett joined the party with Mr. Bassett and Dr. Torrence (28th of September, 1881), and all reached the capital on the second day from Casveen, but all except Mr. Bassett were prostrated with fever. All but one recovered in a few days; that one only after a dangerous illness of three weeks' continuance.

For a better understanding of subsequent events it may be here noted that Mirza Hosein Khan (called Sadr Azam, also Sapr Salar) had recently been removed from office and appointed overseer * of the shrine of Reza at Mashhad, and Mirza Sayed Khan, late overseer of the shrine, had been appointed minister of foreign affairs at Tehran. The former died suddenly at Mashhad in the autumn of 1881. The latter died in Tehran in January, 1884, and was succeeded in office by the Nasr al Mulk. Hosein Khan was noted, as we have stated, for progressive ideas and liberal measures. On the contrary, his successor was considered a bigoted Mussulman.

Soon after the arrival of the reinforcements, Pastor Shamoon of Hamadan—who, as stated, had been arrested and narrowly escaped a scourging—hastened to Tehran. As might be expected, he desired that reparation should

* Mutavalle Bashe.

be made by the authorities for the injury done him. As it did not seem at all probable that the Persian government would take any such view of the action of the governor as the pastor entertained, the pastor being a Persian subject, it was proposed by the mission that if the minister of foreign affairs would issue an order authorizing the return of Shamoon, and requiring the governor there to protect him, no further demands would be made in the case. A request to this effect having been prepared and adopted by the mission, it was transmitted by Mr. Potter to the British minister, and a decisive order was obtained from the Persian minister in the interest of Pastor Shamoon; and thus armed for the future and justified for the past, he returned to Hamadan.

Besides the usual routine business of the annual meeting, some measures were adopted by this session of the Persian mission which are of special interest. It was recommended that the mission be divided, the western part of the country, including the stations of Oroomiah and Tabriz, with their out-stations, to be called the Western Persian Mission, and the eastern and central part of Persia, with the stations of Tehran and Hamadan and their out-stations, to be known as the Eastern Persia Mission. In the course of the following year this recommendation, suggested by Secretary Irving, was approved by the Board of Missions in New York, and the two missions were duly constituted in separate meetings in the fall of 1882. This action was made necessary by the long distances to be traveled between the eastern and western sections of the country in order to attend the annual meetings and to arrange the business of the mission.

In the present lack of missionary forces in the several stations it seemed to be very difficult and inexpedient to spare any one to go to Hamadan. The care of that field was therefore committed, as in the past, to the mission in Tehran, with the recommendation that some one or two of the members should reside in that city. In view of this recommendation, Mr. Hawkes expressed a willingness to go thither, and was therefore appointed to that station. It was with great reluctance that the Tehran station consented to the change, for his services were greatly needed in the capital. He left Tehran in the month of November for his new field of labor, where he was the only American missionary until the arrival in the next year of the missionaries sent expressly for mission-work in that city.

The orders relating to the attendance of Mussulmans at the public services for worship, issued April 2, 1880, by the Persian government, were considered by the mission. The judgment of that body was expressed, in part, in these words: "We ought not and cannot prevent the attendance of Mussulmans on our religious services. In some cases this might be done, but to do so continuously would impose upon us a task difficult if not impossible in itself, and so unworthy of us that it should not be thought of. The order would most naturally apply to the organization of schools and to the systematic gathering by us and our agents of Mussulman congregations. We recognize the obligation to obey God rather than man, but there seems to be warrant for an effort to avert the fury of the secular power. Such effort we may make, in the prayerful hope that Providence will indicate clearly our duty and give ability to discharge it. We recommend, therefore, the following: 1. It is the duty of all our missionaries and native helpers to answer in the spirit of meekness, not of controversy, all who sincerely seek to know the way of life. 2. It is not our duty, nor is it wise, to open schools for Mussulmans at the present time. 3. That it be left to each station to act in view of the aforesaid orders as the providence of God and evident duty may dictate."

A copy of this action was sent to the British minister, for the reason that the orders of the Persian authorities relating to the subject had been received from him. The reply of the minister, dated October 22, 1881, is interesting in several particulars, and is as follows: "If I understand this communication rightly, it is not the intention of the members of the mission generally to prevent Mussulmans from attending your religious services, but all missionaries, native as well as American, are left perfectly free to act as they think best with regard to the attendance or non-attendance of Mussulmans; and you further consider that the prohibitory orders issued by the Persian government, only have reference to the organization of schools for Mussulmans. I feel it to be my duty to call attention to the official memorandum addressed to me by the Persian minister for foreign affairs on the 29th of March, 1881, and communicated by me to Mr. Potter on the 20th of April of that year. That gentleman replied the same day to the effect that he had issued orders directing that no Mussulmans be allowed to attend your religious services and schools. I find it a matter of regret that your committee should now rescind the orders, as by so doing they are incurring a grave responsibility.

"You cannot but be aware that the Persian government have never, for a moment, thought of tolerating a regular school for Mohammedans: the prohibitory orders they have issued are directed not against the opening of schools, a chance they have never even discussed, but against the attendance of individual Mohammedans at religious services. You must bear in mind that Mussulmans here are Persian subjects and amenable to the laws of their country. They render themselves liable to arrest and punishment by attending your services, and it is therefore a serious matter to allow them to do so.

"Considering the sentiments of the Persian government with regard to the proselytism of Mussulmans, I feel it my duty to warn you that should the missionaries here or elsewhere allow Mussulmans to attend their religious services, they will imperil their position in the country, as the government would probably interfere with their work, if they did not even forbid their residing in Persia."

The minister further intimated that he would inform the Persian authorities that the mission declined to observe the orders. In view of this intimation the committee replied, stating that it would be impossible to consider the matter fully and answer at once, and asking that in the mean time no action be taken prejudicial to the interests of the mission.

On the 3d of November an answer was sent by Mr. Bassett, the missionary in charge of the business, such reply having been approved by the mission in Tehran. Its principal points are given in the following extracts from the records: "If we are held responsible for the attendance of Mussulmans at all times and places of our religious worship, then, as must be apparent to every one, there has been put upon us an exceedingly difficult if not impracticable task, as well as one repugnant to our convictions of duty. This is the particular grievance under which we labor, and it is to this that we wish in particular to call the attention of Your Excellency, in the hope that if any action be necessary you will use your influence to obtain a modification of the order, at least in this particular feature of it. While we recognize the power of the Persian government over its own subjects, we wish to put especial emphasis on the fact that it is repugnant to our convictions of right, as well as to our sense of honor, to exclude any persons from our religious meetings. It appears to us, moreover, to be very ungracious on the part of the authorities that they should seek to put us in the attitude of guards over Islam and make us responsible for their own faith."

It was suggested that the mission would post the orders of the Persian government over the chapel-doors if this would be taken as a fulfillment of the order on its part to prevent the attendance of Mohammedans; but to all these expedients the minister replied: "The Persian government having stated clearly that the object they have in view with respect to your chapel services and schools is to prevent Mohammedans from receiving religious instruction from you, it would, in my opinion, be useless to ask them to accept as a fulfillment of their orders the posting of a notice such as you have suggested over the chapel-doors. It may be taken for granted that they will certainly consider their official notification as having been disregarded if they find that Mohammedans are in the habit of attending your services and schools, and that religious instruction is being afforded them. The Shah and his ministers have strongly expressed their determination to carry out the decisions they have taken in this matter with a view to prevent efforts at proselytism amongst Mohammedans, and should any attempt be made in that direction at the present time I believe it will lead to restrictions being placed on your schools and missionary labors here and elsewhere in Persia, if it does not result in objections being raised to your continued residence in the country."

One marked feature of the situation was that, notwithstanding the orders of all parties, Mohammedans were yet attending the religious services in all the mission-stations, and no effort was made to prevent their doing so. The mission was therefore liable to the severe penalties threatened by the minister so long as the orders of the Persian government were not rescinded or modified.

It being evident that nothing could be done through the British legation to modify the order, the mission, after prayerful consideration, adopted, on the 6th of December, the following minute, to wit: "Whereas the British minister, to whom the mission has in years past referred all important matters with the Persian authorities, has recently expressed the opinion that the orders issued in April, 1880, prohibiting the American missionaries from giving instruction to Mussulmans either in school or public assemblies, would be held to be in force by the said authorities, and disregard of such orders would most likely lead to other and great restrictions being put upon our work here and in other places; and whereas there was in 1880, in purport, a promise of obedience to the order made by this station; and whereas sincere and honest dealing with the authorities in such circumstances requires us either to refuse compliance with such orders or to exclude Mussulmans from the religious worship—a task difficult itself and repugnant to our convictions, and which if done promises to create a false impression as to the nature of our work and of our duty to all classes; and whereas said orders had special reference to the religious services on the mission-premises, and should we disregard the clearly expressed opinion of His Excellency we could not reasonably expect his favorable influence in the matter; and whereas the attendance is now largely of Mussulmans; therefore, *Resolved*, That the services in the mission-chapel be discontinued until such time in the providence of God as they may be honestly reopened." The chapel was therefore closed, and the reason therefor was publicly stated to the congregation. It should be added to what is written above touching the orders of the Persian government referred to, that they were issued to the missions of every society in Persia, and so did not relate to the American missions alone.

A communication was now addressed by Mr. Bassett to the Persian minister of foreign affairs, stating the case and asking relief from the order. It was stated that the Persian authorities have control over their own subjects and that to exclude Mohammedans would be contrary to the customs of the missionaries and their religious principles. It was asked, therefore, that the responsibility be transferred to the police, or that the orders be posted on the doors of the chapel. The Persian minister referred the subject to the Shah, as he dared not act independently. On hearing the request, the Shah said, "Let the matter be referred to the police." An order to this effect was sent to the chief of the police from the Persian Foreign Office. As this order is a curious document, I herewith give a translation of it, as follows:

"*To the Count——, Controller of the Order [Nasm] of the City,*
"*One Near the King and Honored:*
"The letter of Mr. Bassett, of the New World, was sent to the Minister of Foreign Affairs. Now, because this matter relates to the order of the city, therefore the letter itself I herewith send, that you should forbid Mussulmans to attend the churches on Sabbath days. What right have the common people [the unlearned] to go to church?

"In the month Rabe ul Aval, 1299 [Jan. 28, A. D. 1882].

"Sealed by the Persian Minister of Foreign Affairs."

This result, though not all that could be desired, was understood to relieve the mission of the necessity of expelling Mohammedans from the chapel or of standing as guards for them. The chapel was therefore reopened for public services on the 30th of January, 1882, and the services have been held at the usual times during subsequent years.

The Rev. J. Lotka, a converted Jew and missionary of the London society referred to above, arrived at Hamadan October 25, 1881, soon after Mr. Hawkes entered the city. The Jews of Hamadan therefore had their earnest expectation fulfilled. The representatives of two missionary societies were now ready to labor for them. The American mission had a nucleus already formed in a church organized and schools established, and twelve years of continuous missionary labor in that city.

In November of this year Mr. Potter, at his own suggestion and with the consent of the mission, removed to the district of Tehran known as the Casveen gate, with a view of being in the settlement of the Armenians and near the chapel in that district. He had charge of the school and chapel services and other work in that quarter. Dr. Torrence opened a dispensary in his own residence on the north side, and was busy in meeting calls for medical services from both Persians and Europeans. He also discharged the duties of treasurer, relieving Mr. Potter of the work of that office. The medical missionary was received with favor at once by all classes of the people: medical skill gave him access to people whom a clergyman could not reach.

Mirza Lazar was now sent to Rasht to take charge of the work there. Owing to delay in making his arrangements for the winter, he did not arrive at that city until December and the opening of the winter. In Tehran prayer-meetings were held once a week by Mrs. Potter on the west side for the benefit of the native women. Special religious services were held in the girls' school, for the benefit of the pupils, by the ladies in charge of the school, and much religious interest was manifested by the older scholars. Services in the chapel on the north side of town were in the charge of Mr. Bassett, who preached also in English to a congregation which met at his residence.

In January, 1882, the school for Jews was reopened by request of the elders of the Jewish colony. The school had now been closed about two years. Besides Baba and the rabbi mentioned as teachers, a converted Jew named Nurillah was employed to teach some of the branches. He was a member of the church in Tehran and attended the king's college. In August, 1883, he departed for London at his own choice and expense, and having letters from members of the mission to the secretary of the Turkish Missions Aid Society. He was detained by sickness on the way, and was in needy circumstances when he entered London. He was kindly received by the secretary of that society, and by him introduced to Mr. Stern, of whom he received instruction. He entered the Hebrew Missionary Training Institution in Palestine Place, London, where he has pursued a course of studies preparatory to the ministry of the gospel. He has spent some of his vacations in connection with the mission to the Jews in Mogadore in Morocco.

The writer of these pages met him in London in 1884, and was much pleased with the evidences of improvement in mind and manners. His progress is most creditable to him, and especially to those who have prepared him for his work.

It was now proposed to change the school of Armenian boys to a boarding-school, owing to the applications received from parents who wished to place their boys in the mission-school. The want of suitable buildings prevented the best arrangement of the school, but a number of boys were placed in Armenian families and aided by an allowance for food and clothing, and others were received as day-scholars. The school was opened in the district of Shimron gate. The pupils of the east-side school were brought to this one, so doing away with the school on that side of the city. Several applications for admission were received from Mohammedans, but being referred to the Persian authorities they were not renewed.

Miss Sarah Bassett returned to the United States on account of ill-health. She left Tehran in April, going by the way of Tabriz, Tiflis and the Black Sea. She was accompanied by Mr. Potter and Miss Schenck to Tabriz. During the absence of these ladies Mrs. Potter had charge of the girls' school. Miss Schenck returned in May, having been absent about one month. She remained with the school in the city during the following summer. On his return from Tabriz, Mr. Potter rented a house adjoining the mission-premises on the north side, and removed to it. The services in the chapel at the Casveen gate were put in charge of the elders of the church, and the school in that place was consolidated with the school on the north side.

As a result of the services in English measures were taken to obtain funds for the erection of a chapel and purchase of land for a cemetery expressly for Protestant foreigners. The Roman Catholics owned a chapel and cemetery used expressly for papal foreigners. The Armenians also had their own place of burial. But no provision had been made for Protestants. A lot of land some four miles from the city, and adjacent to the Roman Catholic burial-ground, had for several years been used, but it was a desolate place and unprotected. The need of effort for foreigners on the part of the mission was felt, not only because of the interest in the religious and general good of the foreigners, but also by reason of the fact that the missionaries, being the only Protestant clergymen in the city, were called upon to officiate at all funerals of Protestants. Requests to bury in our chapel lot were numerous, and threatened to be without end. To refuse was, to say the least, unpleasant to all parties. The proposed chapel was designed to provide for this need of foreign residents. It was a condition of the subscription that the proposed building should be to the satisfaction of the mission and under its control. In the course of a few months the subscription amounted to about twelve hundred dollars, and was paid. With reference to a site, effort was made by the British minister to obtain a grant of land from the Shah. After a delay of some months and the rejection of several objectionable conditions proposed by the authorities, the minister informed the mission that he had accepted a grant of land subject to the following conditions, to wit:

"1. The building should not exceed in size and extent that described in the plans and specifications referred to."

It was manifest to the mission that any such conditions as that could not have emanated from the Shah, as the size and style could be of very little interest to him.

"2. That no children of Mohammedans should be admitted to the chapel; and

"3. That no Mussulmans of any age should be allowed to attend services held in the building."

The mission replied, through Mr. Bassett, that they could not accept the grant on the conditions. The mission had no expectation of using the building for mission purposes, and had no need or desire to open the chapel to Mussulmans or any other Persians, but they were unwilling to submit to any humiliating conditions, especially conditions with reference to which the mission had expressed its feelings and purpose so decisively. The mission proposed that land be *purchased* without condition, but it was stated that the land granted by the Shah had been, by the British minister, tendered to parties of the Church of England in that country, and further aid solicited with a view to an English chaplaincy. The mission therefore asked the subscribers to receive the funds collected. They organized a society, appointed trustees and a building committee and received the amount collected. The mission was thus relieved of any further obligation in the matter. It is to be regretted, however, that the arrangement for the benefit of the foreigners was not completed, for the chapel was not constructed. The English society proceeded in the autumn to lay a foundation for the walls on the land granted by the Shah, but they were informed by the British minister that the Persian authorities would not permit burials to be made within the walls of the city. The trustees therefore, having waited a year, and feeling that as one great object of the undertaking was a cemetery for foreigners, and this was now impracticable, and that they would be defeated in any effort to this end, tendered the funds in hand to the individuals who had subscribed them.

A phenomenon of unusual appearance this year was a total eclipse of the sun. It occurred on the 17th of May, 1882. The period of total obscuration was four minutes, or from 10.28 to 10.32 A. M. The sky was perfectly clear and the stars shone with brilliancy. A bright comet appeared near the sun during the obscuration. Native Persians were much alarmed and very serious. Some of them said they could not understand how we could smile in the day of judgment.

CHAPTER X.

Arrival of Reinforcements—Eastern Persian Mission Constituted—Schools—Theodore Isaac—Services of Public Worship in English—Report of the Girls' School for 1882—Book Department—Medical Department—The Native Church—Death of Usta Abraham—Erection of a New Chapel—The Building Described—Opposition excited by the Amene Sultan—Attempt to Purchase the Mission-Premises by the Amene—The Work in Hamadan—Persecutions—Mirza Sayed Khan—Beginning of the Mission of the United States to Persia—Inquiries concerning the Safety of Citizens of the United States in Persia—Report of the British Foreign Office in Reply—First Appointment under the Act of Congress—Appointment of S. G. W. Benjamin—His Arrival in Persia—His Antecedents and Qualifications—Public Worship in English—Services in Persian—Matters with the Amene Sultan—Affairs in Hamadan—The Secretary of the Legation goes to Hamadan—Attempts of the Old Armenians in Hamadan—Persecutions—Pleasant Episodes—Miss S. Bassett returns to Persia in Company with Miss Sherwood—Summary of the Year's Work—Work for Women, as shown by the Reports of Mrs. Bassett and Mrs. Potter—A Glimpse of the Girls' School, as given by the Report of Miss Bassett—Special Religious Interest in the Winter of 1883-84—Summer Residence and Work—Resignation and Return of Mr. Bassett to America; Reasons therefor—Statements of the Annual Report—Summary of the Year's Work in Hamadan—Summary of Statistics of the Mission—Miss Schenck's Quarterly Report—Miss Bassett's Report of the Year's Work in the Girls' School.

IN the autumn of 1882 the mission was gratified by the arrival of Dr. Alexander and wife, Miss Anna

Montgomery and Miss Cora Bartlett. The three first named had been appointed to Hamadan, and Miss Bartlett to Tehran. They were met at Anzile by Dr. Torrence, and by him escorted to Tehran. They remained here a few days during the organization and session of the Eastern Persian Mission. That mission now met for the first time and adopted a basis of organization and by-laws. The members constituting the mission at the time of organization, named in the order of their connection with the mission to Persia, were—Rev. James Bassett, Mrs. Abigail W. Bassett, Rev. Joseph L. Potter, Miss Sarah J. Bassett (now absent in America), Miss Anna Schenck, Mrs. Harriet Potter, Rev. J. W. Hawkes, Dr. W. W. Torrence, Mrs. Torrence, Dr. E. W. Alexander, Mrs. Alexander, Miss Cora Bartlett and Miss Anna Montgomery.

The schools and religious services were maintained without interruption. The school for Jews was attended by about fifty scholars. The boys' school on the mission premises was taught during the spring and summer by an Armenian named Theodore Isaac, of India. He left that country, where he had received a good education, to attend the University of Cambridge, England. He remained in Tehran until the autumn, and was employed by the mission to teach. He was a very zealous Armenian, and, though willing to teach a Protestant school, would not listen to a Protestant Armenian. He would leave the chapel as soon as one began to preach, because, as he said, they were not ordained. He went on to Cambridge, and thence, in time, to the University of Bonn. From the latter place he wrote in 1886, expressing his readiness to return to Persia, and also indicating a marked change of sentiment with reference to many points of difference with Protestants.

During the winter of 1882-83 the services of religious worship, both in English and Persian, on the mission-premises were conducted by the two clerical missionaries jointly. The attendance on the part of foreigners now, as heretofore, was all that could be expected. Col. Smith, the superintendent of the government of India's telegraph in Persia, gave during many years to these services the encouragement of his presence and influence, and in so doing he was earnestly seconded by his accomplished wife. Mr. Nelson also, superintendent of the Indo-European telegraph in Persia, with his family, was an attendant and reliable friend of the cause, as were also Dr. Baker and others too many to mention in particular.

A few statements from the annual report for 1882 will close the review of that year. The report of the girls' school, made by Miss Schenck, speaks of the religious interest of this year "as more thorough, deep and lasting than at any previous time." Several important points are sought to be attained: 1, To take pupils while very young; 2, to keep the school open during the entire year; 3, to make the English language the medium of instruction. The number of pupils enrolled has been

45. The report of the book department, made by Mr. Potter, shows that 1200 volumes of the Scriptures and parts of the Scriptures have been sold and 433 volumes have been granted, and 617 volumes of text-books sold and 349 volumes granted. Bookrooms have been kept in the cities of Tehran, Rasht, Koom, Zerd and Mashhad. The report of the medical department to May 1, 1882, made by Dr. Torrence, shows that 4539 prescriptions were given, 3352 persons seen for consultation, and the receipts of the department for medical services were T.206.2.09, or $412. A hospital for Persians and Europeans was an object to be attained in the near future. The native church in Tehran had received four members—one a Jew and three Armenians. The total membership was then 29. The contributions of the church amounted to $85. The death of the elder Usta Abraham was a great loss to the church. He was one of the members received at the time of the organization of the church. He was much esteemed for prudence, honesty and industry. He had not been aided by the mission nor was he at any time in its employ. The report of the schools gives those maintained during the year in Tehran. It mentions also the need of a seminary for boys.

In April, 1883, the erection of a new chapel on the mission-premises in the district of Shimron gate was begun. The need of this had long been felt, but the means of construction had not been provided. It was built of burned brick. The height of ceiling was about twenty-two feet. The floor was laid with large tiles, and in three sections raised one above another. The audience-room was seated with well-made pews. The pulpit chairs, of carved wood, were made by the direction of the Persian minister of arts, Jangier Khan, and were given to the mission by him. They were upholstered with crimson velvet. The window-frames and the sash in diamond panes were made by a Persian carpenter and were set with colored glass. The sashes were made in two sections, and turned on perpendicular rods in the centre. A heavy cornice of plaster of Paris extended around the wall beneath the ceiling. There were also three centre-pieces of the same material, and cornices and scrolls above the windows. There was an alcove back of the pulpit, the end of the audience-room having an arch of brick of the width of the platform. The interior walls and ceiling were finished with a white coating of plaster of Paris. This could be well afforded, for gypsum is very abundant in Persia. The structure was completed in the autumn. The walls had been carried to near their full height before any opposition was started. Amene Sultan, the king's chamberlain, was a near neighbor of the mission; he was absent during the summer with the king in Khorasan. His wife, being informed of the building, sent word to stop the work, and caused information to be given to the prince, who appealed to the Shah; but before word could reach Teh-

Interior of New Chapel.   Page 243.

ran the walls were completed. The servants of the prince had ordered the masons to quit the work, and they dared not return until Mr. Bassett himself stood over them and ordered the Mussulmans of the prince's household to attend to their own affairs, and forbade their molesting the masons, refusing to obey any order except that of the Persian Foreign Office delivered by the legation. There was some negotiation, but the Persian minister did not order the walls to be taken down. He gave an order for the completion of the roof. A wall was built on the top of the roof, across the rear, to screen the workmen, so that they could not look into the court of the harem of the prince. For some time the workmen could not go upon the roof without being ordered down by the servants of the sultan. They, being Persians, very naturally feared the displeasure of this man. The Amene had desired to purchase the land on which the chapel had been erected, but the mission could not sell it without great detriment to itself; but it offered to sell all its premises to him on condition of permission being given by the Persian authorities to purchase other land. The Amene, however, seemed to think that he could obtain the property eventually at a low figure. He again sent proposals to purchase when the chapel was completed. He said that he liked the new building and would pay the value of the lot and the cost of the chapel, which was about five thousand dollars. But the mission could not afford to sell its chapel, and the prince renewed his proposals for the purchase of all the premises, saying that he would have to tear down all the buildings except the chapel in case of purchase, as they would be of no use to him. But he was not yet ready to give the full value of the property.

During the winter of 1881–82 the work in Hamadan was carried on without material change. The year 1882 was the first of the two missions, the British and American, in that place, and was a time of great annoyance and of persecution of the Jewish converts. Nor was there any improvement in the year 1883. Mirza Sayed Khan ignored his own orders. In fact, there was no dependence to be placed on his decisions: he observed or evaded them at his own pleasure. The schools were closed and opened, and reclosed and reopened. It was ordered that no one should sell land or building-material to the missionaries in Hamadan or to any foreign missionaries, though building was at the time being carried on by the Protestant mission and the papal mission in Tehran. The opposition was greater, if possible, after the arrival of the American legation than before. A few weeks previous to that the Persian authorities expressed the purpose to leave all matters of inquiry, or not to open any new questions, until the arrival of the American minister.

In the spring of 1882 it was learned that efforts were being made in the United States to obtain an act of

Congress authorizing the appointment of a representative of the government of the United States for Persia. Previous to 1883 the United States had never been represented at the court of Persia. At the time of the war opened on Persia by the Kurds in 1880 inquiries were made by the government of the United States at the British Foreign Office concerning the safety of the citizens of the United States in the country of the Shah. The correspondence includes a reference to the action of the mission taken subsequent to the close of the Kurdish war in 1881, and relates the orders issued by the Persian government touching Mussulmans and the giving of religious instruction to them. In the report of the British Foreign Office there is a partial statement of the reasons assigned for their action, in which it is represented that the missionaries consider it their duty "to obey God rather than man," and the condition of the missionaries in consequence of their action is said to be "critical," so much so as to seem to justify a telegram from the Department of State in Washington to the minister of the United States in London, expressing the hope that Her Majesty's representatives would continue to afford protection to the missionaries as heretofore. All this was the result of the report of the action of the mission to the British Foreign Office by Mr. Ronald Thomson, the British minister in Tehran, while the missionaries had to appeal to the Shah himself for protection from those measures to which the British minister himself was a party. The representations made by Mr. Thomson were an important factor in the influences leading to the establishment of a mission of the United States government in Persia. The reason given for the mission was "the protection of American citizens" in Persia. The results were very acceptable to those citizens, and the Americans resident in Persia have occasion for gratitude to the people in America who had their interest so much at heart as to adopt measures for their protection—a favor which the missionaries would have been very reluctant to claim.

The first appointment under the act of Congress was that of Rev. H. H. Jessup, D. D., of Syria. It is fairly presumed that no one acquainted with Dr. Jessup would have thought that he would accept the appointment. It may be believed that it was sought for him by interested friends as an act of courtesy in their anxiety to do him honor.

On the declination of the appointment by Dr. Jessup, Mr. S. G. W. Benjamin was appointed minister resident and consul-general at the court of the Shah. He arrived with his wife and daughter at Anzile in the month of May, 1883, and was escorted to the capital with the usual honors and by a special messenger of the Shah. He was formally received in the capital on the 9th of June, the king having delayed his own departure for Mashhad to do him honor. His Majesty departed on the same day for the eastern border of his dominions, ostensibly, it is said, to pay his devotions at the shrine of Reza, but really to investigate certain questions about the boundaries as they would be affected by the operations of the Russians in Turkistan.

Mr. Benjamin is the son of the Rev. Nathan Benjamin, a missionary appointed in 1836 by the American Board to Athos in Greece, and later to Athens and Constantinople. The early associations of the minister were such, therefore, as to make him a friend of missionaries. Well acquainted with the French and Turkish languages and the character and customs of Orientals, a man of literary culture, he was well fitted by these and other qualifications for the position to which he had been appointed.

Mr. Benjamin, as well as Col. Smith and other persons, was desirous that services in English should be held in the new chapel on Sabbath afternoons. They were therefore begun and maintained during the usual time of residence in the city. Later in the season, by special arrangement with the members of the American and British legations, the morning services of the Church of England were read by Mr. Bassett and a sermon was preached by him. The members of the British legation contracted to pay during the season the sum of about $150, which was duly paid to the treasurer of the mission.

The services in Persian were conducted by the two missionaries, each officiating on alternate Sabbaths. A Sabbath-school for Persians was sustained by good attendance, also a prayer-meeting on Fridays in Persian.

The demands of the Amene Sultan and business matters relating to Hamadan were referred to Mr. Benjamin. It was demanded of the Amene that he should fill up with brickwork the windows which he had constructed to overlook the mission-premises. This business fell to the Persian minister of foreign affairs. But Mirza Sayed Khan was fruitful in expedients for avoiding the points at issue, and he feared the influence of the Amene. The windows, however, were in time closed through the efforts of the legation. Matters with the authorities in Hamadan went on from bad to worse until the spring and summer of 1884. In the winter of 1883–84 the Christian Jews were greatly annoyed, as were also the missionaries in that city. Owing to the difficulty experienced in obtaining any redress of wrongs from Mirza Sayed Khan, the minister sent his secretary, Mr. Keun, to Hamadan to consult with authorities there. Some of the Jewish converts had been beaten, fined and imprisoned for persisting in serving the missionaries, contrary to the order of the Persian authorities. In the fall of 1883 the Armenians of Shevarin attempted to obtain possession of the church in Hamadan. The farashes entered the building and took out the benches and other property belonging to the missionaries, and closed the doors of the church. The representative of the legation could obtain no concessions from the authorities. The prince-governor had returned to Tehran, leaving affairs in the management of his son, a mere lad. The secretary called to his aid the farashes of the governor and arrested some of the offenders, and caused the schools to be opened, but they were closed as soon as he left the city. The farashes put a lock and seal on the doors of the building used for a school for Jews. A school for Armenian girls in the care of Miss Montgomery was not molested. In spite of these annoyances, though not permitted to build, the missionaries were suffered to purchase residences for their own use. Mirza Sayed Khan died in the spring of 1884. It was hoped that his successor would be more liberal and efficient. Mr. Benjamin presented to him a strong protest against the acts of the authorities in Hamadan, and demanded indemnity and the removal of some of the officials of that city; but the new Persian minister very deliberately composed a reply charging that the missionaries had violated treaty stipulations. These charges were, however, withdrawn, for he soon thereafter ordered indemnity to be taken from the Armenians who had caused the church-furniture to be seized and the church closed.

It must not be thought that there were no pleasant phases of the mission-work and life in Hamadan. The following extract from a letter written by Dr. Alexander, under the date of February 9, 1883, shows that there were some pleasant episodes in the course of affairs:

"We were all to the prince's Wednesday night, and the big man of Shevarin has sent his carriage to take us out to his place for the evening; so you see we do not live in constant storms. God is always kind, and makes it pleasant for us here."

In the month of October, Miss S. Bassett returned from America in company with Miss Sherwood, appointed to Tehran, but, owing to the fact that Miss Montgomery was without an associate in the women's work in Hamadan, Miss Sherwood was a few months later transferred to the mission in that city. In the fall of the following year she married the Rev. J. W. Hawkes of Hamadan. On the arrival of the ladies at Anzile they were met by Mr. Potter to escort them to Tehran.

A few statements gleaned from the annual report of this year give a concise account of the year's work. Two schools were maintained in Tehran throughout the year. One of these, situated near the Casveen gate, has been attended by about 25 children of Armenians. Of this number, 12 have been assisted by allowances for food and clothing, and 2 are orphans and 5 are half-orphans. This school is designed to be, as soon as possible, a boarding-school for boys. Two thousand tomans were asked for the purpose of erecting a suitable building. The studies pursued are in Persian, English and Armenian. The second school is that for the children of Jews. The average attendance has been 40. The languages employed in instruction are Hebrew, Persian and English. The New Testament in Persian is used as a text-

Hut and Booth near Rasht. Page 253.

book, and the Catechism is learned. The school in Rasht has been attended by 20 pupils. The congregation of native Persians was removed to the west side of Tehran, owing to changes to be made in the buildings occupied hitherto on the north side of town. The services were attended by Jews, Armenians and Mohammedans. The Persian authorities have not interfered with the attendance. The native church has experienced no marked change. Land for a cemetery has been purchased by the church. The report mentions the need of a well-qualified native pastor. It mentions also the subscription for a chapel and cemetery for foreigners, and the erection on the mission-premises of a new chapel capable of seating three hundred people. The interest in Rasht culminated in the organization (October 16, 1883) of a church in that city and under the care of Mirza Lazar. The collections in Rasht have amounted to about $64. Priest Megerditch has resided and labored in Bohmain and its vicinity. The arrival of a legation of the United States is mentioned as a propitious event, relieving the mission of the greater part of the usual business with the Persian authorities.

The work for Persian women may be shown by extracts from the reports made by the ladies in charge of the different departments of that work. Mrs. Bassett began to hold meetings with Jewish women this year in the Jewish quarter of the city. Concerning this, under date of November 13, 1883, she writes: "I began meetings in the Jewish quarter in the month of November. Met at the house of Mirza Baba, who is the teacher of the Jews' boys' school, with an attendance of 24 women and girls. They seemed greatly pleased that I should meet them once every week and endeavor to show them the way of life. The number increased gradually week by week, also the interest. I said to the women and little girls the next week after the meeting, I would meet all who wished to learn to read. When the time came I found eight or ten girls ready for their lesson. The women thought they were too old to commence to learn to read. But before I had finished with the little ones they were looking over my shoulder at the letters, and seemed much interested. Their ignorance and degradation are very great. It seems strange to them that we should read. They need to be taught of the better life. I hope this winter we may hear many of them inquiring what they shall do to be saved. They manifested a great deal of interest, and were generally regular in their attendance, bringing some new one with them nearly every time. They often come to see me."

Mrs. Potter writes, under date of October, 1883, of her work among Armenian women: "Naturally, the work commences and the interest centres among those who are members of our church; and, very happily, nearly all of these live in one quarter of the city, near each other. Early in the fall we called upon them preparatory to starting a weekly prayer-meeting to be

Armenian Mother and Son.   Page 257.

held from house to house. Most of the women expressed great willingness to attend and take part in such a service, promising to do all they could to sustain it. Looking back now over the months, including all the meetings in one glance, I think I can say they have kept their word. If there has been disappointment at one time, there has been encouragement at another. A bright spot that I may mention is the interest shown by one woman, a sister of the wife of one of our helpers. Her husband is engaged in making and selling wine, and is so much opposed to us and to Protestantism as to have even destroyed his wife's Testament and hymn-book some few years ago, forbidding her to have anything to do with us. Still, she managed to get other books, and under pretence of visiting her friends would frequently come to the preaching services. But last winter she took a bolder stand, and urged that we should hold our prayer-meeting at her home in its turn. We saw with great delight her desire to hear and learn the truth. This little cluster of praying women met together regularly each week from November until May, with one or two exceptions when bad weather or sickness prevented, and we think there was a perceptible spiritual growth among them, though we cannot report many brought into the kingdom of those entirely unacquainted with its truths.

"At the beginning of February a meeting was opened in another Armenian quarter of the city, distant fully two miles from the missionary's house, a considerable part of the way being through the bazars. But this difficulty was the least of all to be surmounted, a far greater one being to gain access to the hearts of the women themselves, or even to find any of them willing to listen. Before attempting the service we called among them and asked whether they would like to have it. With the native politeness and (shall I say it?) lack of sincerity, their answers to us were very favorable. But on the day appointed for the first meeting they sent us a message to the effect that, word having been passed about, no one was ready to come. Still, we persevered in going, and were encouraged by being able to gather together eleven persons; and the average attendance continued to be nearly this number during the three months, notwithstanding the prejudices against us which were plainly felt to exist, and the influence of those who adhered strongly to the old faith.

"Sanam, a native Christian woman, for some years a pupil in our girls' school, accompanied us to these meetings, partly because we feel that she is qualified for evangelical work and are desirous to help her take it up, and also that she might introduce us into homes where we were unacquainted. She proved to be of great assistance in reading the portions of Scripture selected for the day, leading in prayer, helping to sing the hymns and sometimes speaking a few words. After the meeting we frequently went together to call upon some one whom she knew and invite her to attend the following week.

"An incident which occurred one day may serve to show how little heart some of them had in the matter, and how well satisfied they were with their own spiritual condition. We were waiting for the women to assemble when an old woman came in who with her daughter had repeatedly been invited to the service. After the usual salutations, Sanam inquired for the daughter. Raising her voice to a high tone, the mother burst forth with, 'Why should she come? What shall she come for? Is the lady going to give us MONEY?' (This last word she fairly shouted.) Then turning to me with many gestures, still speaking at the top of her voice, she said, 'Money! money! Give us money; that is what we want. It is the beginning of all things; we cannot have clothes or rice or anything without money; give us that, lady.' She was told that if she would listen she would receive something still better than money, but her cry was still the same, and she continued to shout and gesticulate until the others, coming in, so took my attention that she was obliged to stop. Now, all this was half in jest, but it showed most plainly the woman's real feelings, that money was worth more to her than any teaching; nor could she be convinced that there was anything better to desire, though plainly told that one who was nearing the grave, as she was, should be far more careful for her soul's welfare than for getting money, which she could not take with her. Also, a poor woman coming in with tears running down her cheeks, carrying a sick child in her arms and having left a husband at home crazy with delirium tremens, afforded a good opportunity to show her that there are troubles which even money cannot alleviate. But it was all of no effect, for the old woman left the house as soon as she saw me open my Testament."

A glimpse of the interior of the girls' school is given in the following quarterly report made by Miss Bartlett. It represents the last quarter of the year 1882, but virtually the first quarter of the mission-work for 1883:

"On the 4th of October, 1882, I entered our schoolroom for the first time, and I wish I could tell you how pleased I was with our black-haired, black-eyed girls. Though I have been only a short time in Persia, would you, dear home-friends, like to hear some of my first impressions of our work? It seems to me that the harvest of Persia is not yet ripe for the gathering of golden sheaves, but that much of the toilsome, weary work of preparation and seed-sowing still remains to be done. But in our own special field, the girls' school, much of this harder foundation-work has been accomplished by such self-denying labors as some of us will never know.

"The school is not yet running like clock-work, for there are not enough laborers to keep all the parts thoroughly oiled; but many things mark steady improvement. We have enrolled during this last quarter 34 names. This is not many, we know, but it is sufficient increase over former years to show that the balance tips

Carepet and his Wife Victoria. Page 263.

to the right side. Of this number, 10 are *contract*-girls; that is, girls whose parents or relatives have signed their names to a written agreement, thus promising them to us for a term of years, not less than five. In this way we gain complete control over them, and they are not merely *scholars*, but our children, to be cared for in *every particular*. No, we are not proud of them *now*, but we hope to be some day, when they go forth to throw the light of Christian womanhood into the darkness of their surroundings.

"We were glad to welcome Sanam and Victoria back as day-scholars. They were married and left us three years ago, and have now returned, each seeking work for hands and hearts left idle and empty by the death of their little ones. Their husbands are two of our most promising helpers, and we rejoice not only to see these girls striving to keep step with them, but also because we think it will have some influence against the horrid custom of early marriage which steals away our girls so soon.

"But the company that gathers in our schoolroom would not be complete without mention of the two women of our household. One of these, Sushan, is an earnest Christian, a member of the church, who has come through much trouble to find everlasting peace. We hear with gladness of her meetings and talks with the girls, for we think her influence most salutary. If I could show you the numerous pairs of little native stockings out at toes and heels, the gaping holes made by the week's wear and tear, the piles of plain sewing waiting to be done, you could easily guess her occupation. During this quarter we received the first money ever paid by the father of one of our girls for current expenses.

"As our earnest desire is that the girls may become earnest Christians while with us, much attention is given to religious instruction, Miss Schenck and Mrs. Potter each having a daily Bible-class and afternoon meeting on Sabbath. I cannot help in this way now, so I have several English classes, hoping that if I fail to learn Armenian we may still be able to talk a little. Mrs. Potter and I have spent a good many hours over the sewing, but if you should visit us you might not believe it unless you should give long enough notice for the girls to don their Sunday dresses. I grumble a good deal because the parents ask for their children so often, and when once out of the house we have no idea when we shall see them again; but Miss Schenck can laugh at this annoyance, it is so much less than formerly.

"The week of prayer called us for a while from our usual duties, and besides special services held in the little prayer-room and on the other side of the city we had several meetings in our schoolroom. We exerted ourselves to keep the 14 girls who remained with us during the holidays both busy and happy. To each was given a new dress, and they sewed industriously and merrily over them, thus occupying the days, and in the evenings we entertained them with games. We prepared for their Christmas, the 18th of January, a little Christmas-tree, which really looked quite pretty trimmed up with popcorn, fancy bags filled with candy, oranges, picture-books, English and Armenian Testaments, Bibles and a nice woolen dress for each of the women. Plenty of time was given them to enjoy it, while we passed bountiful refreshments of oranges, popcorn balls, candy, nuts and figs. The delight of the children well repaid us for our trouble. Last week the day of prayer for schools was observed, and nearly the whole day was spent in prayer and praise. We long very much to have it a marked day in our school, that the girls may learn to look forward to it. Some of our girls are Christians, we hope, but we need, more than I can tell you, an outpouring of the Spirit."

During the winter of 1883–84 special religious interest prevailed in the girls' school and in the congregation. The attendance at the public services on Fridays and Sabbaths was larger than ever before. The number present was often as many as one hundred and fifty. Of these as many as fifty or sixty were Mohammedans, some were Jews and many were Armenians. As a result of the interest, on the 14th of May, 1884, fourteen persons united with the church in Tehran. Five of these were pupils of the girls' school.

During the summer Mr. Potter and Dr. Torrence with

their families resided in Gulhek, the summer retreat of the British legation; Mr. Bassett and family and the girls' school, with the ladies in charge, occupied premises in the village of Tajreesh, at the place called Aseaub, or the Mill. Mr. Bassett remained here until the 24th of August, 1884, preaching on Sabbaths in the city to the native church and congregation. On the day mentioned he and his family departed for the United States, he having some months previously resigned his connection with the Board and the mission, to take effect this year. The reasons leading him to take this step were, first, the educational wants of his family—wants which could not be met in Persia; and, secondly, the inadequate support furnished under the regulations of the Board. This inadequacy has since been shown by the fact that the salaries of the missionaries in Persia have been very materially increased since he left the field. At this time a reinforcement for the mission was expected to arrive in the fall.

A few statements gathered from the annual report of the mission with reference to the mission-work of the year 1884 will be pertinent and complete the record up to this date.

The Rev. T. J. Porter and wife arrived at Tehran on the 23d of October. He took charge of the services of public worship in English for the remainder of the year. The Sabbath-school was continued during the winter and spring and until the hot season, when it was dismissed until fall. The average attendance of the Sabbath-school had been 85. The total number of members received to the Tehran church from the time of organization in 1876 had been, including those persons received this year, 57. The membership at this date was 38, giving a loss of 19 by removals and deaths since the organization. The contributions from all sources amounted to $419. Weekly prayer-meetings for native women were held by Mrs. Potter in the Armenian quarter of town, and a monthly social gathering of native women was held in the fall at the houses of Mrs. Potter and Mrs. Torrence alternately. The year was a prosperous one in the girls' school. The whole number enrolled was 40; the average attendance of pupils, 31. The school for Jewish girls numbered 15 pupils. The total number of scholars in the mission-schools was 146. Dr. Torrence reported the number of patients at the dispensary during the year to be 2500. In the latter part of the year the dispensary was removed to another quarter of the town, owing to the danger to the mission families from infectious diseases. Three books are reported as having been published in the course of the year—namely: *The Shorter Catechism*, translated by Mr. Bassett, a 16mo volume of 65 pages; a new enlarged edition of hymns in Persian, translated by Mr. Bassett, a 16mo volume of 67 pages; *Pilgrim's Progress*, translated by J. L. Potter, with notes and index. Each copy contains six full-page wood-cuts, the sheets being furnished at cost by the Presbyterian Board of Publication. The sales of Scriptures were 1214 volumes, and of religious text-books 418 volumes.

A summary of the year's work in Hamadan is made in the report of that mission, the substance of which is given as follows:

"The mission-work at Hamadan has been impeded during the past year by various forms of opposition on the part of all classes—Moslems, Armenians and Jews. Notwithstanding the forces working against them, however, the missionaries have not only held their position, but have made substantial progress in their work.

"As heretofore, two services have been held each Sabbath in the Armenian quarter of the city without interruption, the aged Nestorian pastor and Mr. Hawkes conducting the services. The church-building hitherto occupied for these services—which, by the way, is dark, dilapidated and uncomfortable—was claimed by the old Armenians, and through the enmity of certain influential men at the capital was given over by the authorities to them. The Protestants have since worshiped in private houses. 'We have made this,' writes Mr. Hawkes, 'the occasion of a petition to the Shah for permission to build a new chapel, and the last mail brings word that he has granted the petition and made a contribution of 400 tomans toward the erection of the building. The prince-governor came to see the chosen location, approved of it, and ordered that work should commence about the 1st of April. We hope it will be completed before next winter.' The Sunday-school has been kept up, with 110 names on the roll and an average attendance of 60. Services among the Jews have been attended by only a small number, as the people have been in constant fear of persecution. To lessen their fears, Pastor Shimon has taken a house in the midst of their homes, and, having accommodations in his dwelling both for preaching services and a girls' school, it is hoped that they both may be carried on without interruption.

"The girls' school in the Armenian quarter is the only one that has been allowed to continue its course undisturbed through the various persecutions of the year. Fifty-six have been in attendance. Since the marriage of Miss Sherwood to the Rev. Mr. Hawkes, Miss Montgomery, her associate in the school, has received into the building ten boarders. Her labors in the supervision of such a school, requiring unremitting attention upon her part, while, at the same time, she is prosecuting the study of both Persian and Armenian, it will be readily seen, must be very arduous.

"The boys' high school has been sadly interrupted, being several times closed by government order. The Jewish boys have thus lost much time, and the Armenians, although generally keeping up their studies, have not made the progress they should have done. Dr. and Mrs. Alexander have opened a boarding department for the boys in an unoccupied room in their house. They have had six under their care. Another school, for Jewish boys only, has been started during the past year. There are in it some 50 boys, but the disturbances prevailing have had their influence upon this also.

"A school started by Mrs. Alexander for girls in the Jewish quarter was soon stopped by the government. The number enrolled reached 25. The immediate cause of the closing was a prayer-meeting started in the same room at the urgent request of the neighbors. It immediately stirred up the prejudices of the leading Jews.

"Dr. E. W. Alexander has rendered valuable service to the many natives who have sought his help through the year, notwithstanding the violent opposition of the native doctors, who, while secretly admitting the virtue of foreign medicine, say that they must shut out the foreigners as long as possible. Both he and Mrs. Alexander claim our deep sympathy because of the successive forms of sickness with which she has been afflicted, having long suffered from a low form of fever and also from an attack of smallpox, which was at one time raging in the city. The health of the other missionaries has been almost uninterruptedly good."

A review of the foregoing statements shows that the total number of pupils in all the schools of the Eastern Persia Mission at this date was 276, including 15 scholars in the school in Rasht. Regular congregations were sustained in three cities and one village. The number of congregations was 6, with an average attendance of about 175 in all. The Sabbath-school attendants numbered about 250. The congregation of English-speaking people is not included in this estimate.

Miss Schenck, in her quarterly report of April, 1884, writes of the girls' school:

"Several of our girls have been Christians, no doubt, for some length of time, and it is our joy to rejoice in recognizing their gradual quiet growth into an ever higher degree of piety, as evidenced in the formation of Christian character, the questions of conscience from thoughtful ones, the response from the face indicative of unexpressed concern within, and the unhidden, interested anxiety for the spiritual condition of parents still ignorant of the true spirit and intent of Christ's gospel.

"Some of the girls are touchingly moved to take the occasion of calls [of parents] on reception-day to read the Bible to their parents, unabashed by the presence of others. One dear child even followed up this reading by putting in her father's pocket a previously-written note for him to spell out at his leisure at home, and, we trust, to be moved by its plain words and bold—for a daughter in this land to say to her father—to be concerned for his own soul as his child is for it.

"Other girls, more recently entered, seem almost immediately to show in face and conduct an acquiescence in the teachings and a readiness to assume their duty, as shown to them in God's word, before they are able to read it for themselves. These Christian girls are with us, and growing in their Christian life. As we pray regularly right through the roll for them, one by one, as is our custom, our faith grasps the promises of God for them.

"But these poor children are not blessed with pious parents—far from it. Some of these, especially the mothers, are wicked in heart and life, and they wish and expect their daughters to be the same. Indeed, the only motive of some in putting their girls with us is the hope that it may prove a time of preparation for them to gain money by selling them without marriage. We may be brought to face the fact that neither we nor the girl can stand against the power of a wicked mother to dispose as she will of her child.

"Can you, in view of these facts, appreciate the perplexity with which we meet a question that is much in our thoughts and prayers—that of receiving the girls into church-membership? This in Christian lands is a simple, straightforward matter, the first presented and acknowledged duty and privilege of a convert to claim the blessings of full membership in the visible Church. Duty here, in such cases, is a complicated question. Who is wise enough to decide it? Since children of God may be saved out of the Church, is it expedient to risk bringing reproach upon the Church, rather than wait a few years, if need be, for developments in their future life? Our experience leads us to choose the safer course of not hurrying them into the churches.

"Many show much interest in their lessons. The

progress in most cases is commendable. Some, from not having any idea how to hold a pen, have in a short time learned to write a fair hand. But they are chips of the old blocks, after all, and have some queer ways to which they cling, such as putting away their books, bread and treasures under the carpets (carpets here are not tacked down) and tying up clothing in a big cloth, though nice little chests and shelves and hooks are provided for their use. We are still suffering the inconvenience of having no desks for our schoolroom.

"Having three lady-teachers present this winter has enabled us to make marked progress in English instruction. The examination was entirely in English, except a Catechism of Bible history in Armenian. The classes were practical, and mental arithmetic, algebra, geography, dictation and grammar, with children's motion-songs interspersed. Rewards of English Bibles were given to six girls for committing the Catechism for Young Children in English. At present most of the teaching is oral and without books, though we expect gradually, as they get more command of the language, to have them use books.

"One of our church elders has a weekly class of the older girls, the time of which he is now employing in teaching and explaining the Church covenant.

"Our household has been greatly blessed in health during this winter of unusual sickness and frequent death. Indeed, with grateful hearts we record the fact that our school has never been visited with a really serious case of illness. Did Easter come oftener than once a year, we fear such would cease to be true, for the quantity of eggs that a school full of girls can boil, color and otherwise dispose of is enough to do away with all hope of good health for some time to come. However, our experience with picnics as an antidote for hard-boiled eggs has so far proved successful. This year we tried an extra large dose, going a mile outside of the city—not to such woods, however, as American children have for picnicking. Oh no! Woods are unknown about Tehran. But the Shah and such other men as are rich enough plant gardens in the desert, and build high mud walls around them, and dig ditches through which the water is brought down from the mountains to water the garden, and so trees are coaxed to grow. And sometimes, by paying the gardener who takes care of it, we can get permission, as we did this time, to spend the day in his garden. But he looks rather nonplussed when he unlocks and opens the great gate, and thinks what injury all these forty folk and nine donkeys are likely to do to his fruit trees if permitted to run wild in his garden. So the girls, instead of having entire freedom, have to be cautioned to be careful and play in the broad paths. But what with getting up their swing and using it to their hearts' content, and eating several lunches, and the fun of riding the donkeys up and down through the garden, and some riding while the others walked back to the city, as we had gone out in the morning, we were about as tired a set as if our picnic had been in the old orthodox American style.

"We are indebted for two boxes from Erie Presbyterial Society, and could the kind friends know the help and impulse given to our social hour, as shown in the greater amount and better work accomplished since its arrival, they would be sufficiently repaid and thanked.

"The gift of a magic-lantern from Iowa has been much appreciated by the girls.

"Two boxes with very acceptable contents and of most helpful character were also received from different bands and auxiliaries of the Philadelphia society. Could the makers of that clothing see the neat appearance of our girls, and appreciate the actual labor saved to us by their sending it all ready to put on, they would understand how we prize their boxes, better than by any words we can write."

The year's work of the girls' school is reviewed by Miss Sarah Bassett in the annual report, under date of October, 1884, as follows:

"It is my duty as well as pleasure to review the past year, not only for our own benefit, but also that our friends may know what we have striven to accomplish.

"The last day of October, 1883, found me again in Tehran, after an absence of eighteen months, ready and glad to resume my share of duties which had rested heavily on shoulders not able to carry such a burden, however willing they might be.

"Classes were soon formed, and during the winter there were daily recitations in arithmetic, both mental and practical, algebra, geography, reading, writing, grammar and dictation in the English language, while the Bible was studied in the Armenian. Afternoons were spent by the girls in studying Armenian and Persian with a native teacher, and part of the year French. Evenings were devoted to what was called the English social hour, at which time fancy-work was taught and English spoken.

"The week of prayer was duly observed, besides the regular public services, which the girls were able to attend only part of the time, owing to the rain and to the meetings being on the west side of the city some distance from us: the missionaries each met the girls in the schoolroom and pointed out the way of life in plain language, to which the girls listened attentively and after-results proved that they were profited thereby.

"The Armenian New Year and Christmas were each noticed and celebrated in a way to delight the hearts of the children, especially the latter day. Upon it the girls were invited to see a beautiful tree the ladies had dressed for their pleasure with lovely gifts sent by kind friends in the home-land for such occasions. The missionaries, with our United States minister, his wife and daughter, were invited to witness the giving of the gifts to the girls. It was very gratifying to have Mr. and Mrs. Benjamin express so heartily their surprise and pleasure in what they saw to commend in our school. Such times have their mission of encouragement to us, marking as they do our growth and progress in numbers, manner and appearance.

"The day of prayer for schools was not forgotten, but was observed by religious exercises from morning until evening, and, from studying the faces of the pupils, we could not but feel they were thoughtfully and earnestly striving to make the day one which would never be forgotten.

"May 18th our hearts were gladdened by seeing five of our girls unite with the church, thus acknowledging their love for the Saviour and desire to glorify him. Very earnestly we pray that their example may be such as will lead their friends and schoolmates to Christ.

"During May and in July the girls were taken for picnics to gardens near the city. In this way we strive to give them the change they need and still keep them with us. The wet spring, followed by unusually cool summer weather, made us hopeful of more than usual comfort during the hot months, and that we would be able to continue the lessons and accomplish much sewing. But early in July there were indications of poor health among the girls, which resulted in some serious illness and interfered with our plans. Among the cases very like scarlet fever one case of smallpox was developed, which was immediately removed to a rented house, with nurses hired to care for her. The remaining pupils were sent to a garden not far from the city, with two elders and their families, to await results. After fifteen days' quarantine and no one being ill, we all removed to a garden at Tajreesh. July 29th, after an illness of three weeks, Aroosiag Hargobian died. She was one of our brightest and best little girls, loved by all her schoolmates as well as her teachers.

"The two months in the country were spent busily sewing, and during that time four hundred yards of cloth and muslin were transformed into one hundred and forty garments. Some of the girls were taught to cut and fit and to sew on the sewing-machine, thus being of use to us, and preparing them, should it be necessary, to earn their livelihood in this city, where machines are becoming abundant.

"Our whole number of pupils enrolled during the year has been 40, with an average attendance of 32. We were made the recipients during the year of four boxes, filled with clothing and materials for our work in the social hour, from friends in the home-land. Thus the year has passed with all its trials and pleasures, and we have entered upon a new year with 34 names enrolled and new studies begun."

CHAPTER XI.

Methods of Mission-Labor in Persia, especially Eastern Persia—Methods Modified by the Condition of the People—The Romantic Method—Finding a Congregation—Henry Martyn's Experience—Street-Preaching not Attempted in Mohammedan Villages—Practicable in Christian Villages—Obstacles to Gathering Congregations—Intolerance of Islam—Opposition of the Priests—Too Sensitive a Conscience—Time-honored Religions—Protestantism too Honest—Power and Futility of Controversy—Other Methods Essential—Interested and Disinterested Motives—Desire for Education and Power of Schools—Permanent Congregations, how Formed—Difficulty in the Way of Obtaining Native Preachers—Nestorian Preachers—Armenians of Eastern Persia—Assistants to be Trained—Religious Services—Persians accustomed to Public Worship—Habits of Reverence—Preaching—Music—Influence of Sacred Song—The Organ—Matter of Preaching—Doctrines of Religion—Objectionable Doctrines—The Ale Allahees—Effect of the Peculiarities of the Persian Religion on the Relations of Persians to Christianity—Imitation of Christian Doctrine, and Assumptions—Resemblance to Rome—Revulsion from Rome—Conflict of the Gospel and Sheahism—Method of Successful Approach—Preparatory Instruction of Converts—Circulation of the Scriptures—Instances of the Influence of the Bible—The Circulation of Other Books—Pfander's Works—Books in the Armenian Language—Kind of Books Needed—Use of Medical Missions—Special Efforts for Persian Women by Christian Women.

THE methods of missionary labor are necessarily modified in different lands by the condition of the people to whom that labor is directed. There are marked resemblances, however, in the methods followed in all lands. Social and religious laws, climate, language, and even the material resources of the people, affect in some way the agencies for reaching the populace. One of the first questions proposed in every new mission-field is, "How shall a congregation be obtained?" The question is pretty well understood by all who are informed on mission-work. But it is not always suggested as one that may have any perplexity about it. In the old fields the congregations are gathered. But in a new work, like that to be opened in Tehran, the question remained to be answered. The romantic notion of early missionary efforts had no place here, for the intolerant spirit and laws of the country are too evident for any one to be deceived or to remain in doubt as to the practicability of that idea. The notion once prevailed that the missionary had only to acquire the language of the country, and then go upon the street to preach, in order to get hearers. There are many young men entering the foreign work who seem not to have given thought to this subject, and are not undeceived until they reach a foreign shore and undertake to find their congregations. Henry Martyn writes of the great difference between his fond expectation of having crowds of poor Indians to hear him preach, and the reality as he found it in his labors. There are some countries where the missionary may regularly go to the market or the street and preach, but he cannot do so in Tehran nor in any other city of a mixed population in Persia. It has not been attempted, so far as I know, by any one to preach in the bazar or maidon. The fact that it has not been done is evidence of some good reason why it has not been attempted. This method may possibly be practicable in the near future, but has not been in the past, and is thought to be impracticable now. The reason that it is so is the intolerance and fanaticism of the Mohammedans. This method is entirely practicable in the Armenian and Jewish communities, but where there is a Mohammedan population any public effort of this sort would be understood by mullahs and by priests to be a bold attempt to proselyte. No one could pursue this course without violence to the common law of the land nor without exciting a mob. It is possible that one or two efforts on this plan might be successful, but no one acquainted with the people would have any hope of being able to keep up the practice of preaching in the public places. In every instance where the missionary meets the people for the first time, he is certain to have an audience drawn by the powerful motive of curiosity. But when the preaching has ceased to be a new thing, the hearers will be wanting. There are many reasons why this is so. In the beginning of effort among the old Christian sects the priests and bishops usually oppose and intimidate their people. The priests of all orders have great power. They can refuse to administer the sacraments and can inflict stripes. Until recently they could imprison the disobedient. They can threaten the erring with excommunication in this life and with the pains of hell for ever. The effect of their threats is invariably to prevent the greater part of their people from affiliating with Protestants. So far as gatherings of Mohammedans are concerned with mission-labor, these are regarded as wholly impracticable. I have never seen a Mohammedan who would think of resisting the order of a mujtaheed with reference to adherence to Christians. Even converted Mohammedans would consider it necessary to flee for their lives should they receive any intimation from a mujtaheed that they were suspected of entertaining the sentiments of Christians.

But there is a more potent influence to overcome than the intolerance and violence of mujtaheeds and priests. It is the natural dislike of the reproof of sin, a disquieted conscience. A Persian who frequently came to our chapel suddenly ceased to attend the services. I asked him why it was that one who had appeared so attentive for a time should stay away so long. He replied, "That which I hear makes me feel uncomfortable; it makes me dissatisfied with myself and my religion, and therefore I stay away."

It is one marked feature of the first efforts for these people, while as yet a congregation and church are unformed, that so many persons never come to hear the word more than two or three times. Crowds will come so long as they fail to perceive the exact object of the preacher. As soon as they begin to understand the spiritual and moral nature of the requirements made, they begin to be offended. How could we reasonably look for any other result? They find all their old grounds of trust dissolving; their good works are seen to be of no account. They find that they must undergo a terrible trial: they have to meet the scorn and opposition of the priests to whom they have from infancy been trained to look for instruction, and who are believed to possess the "power of opening and closing the gates of heaven;" they have to meet a great deal of social ostracism; the new belief divides the house and sets the members of the household one against another. But a more powerful motive than these considerations remains, strong as the other facts may be: it is the fact that they must give up their own time-honored and cherished religion and their only hope of salvation. Said a Persian mullah who had considered the alternative presented by our preaching: "I see that if I become a Christian I must cease to believe in Mohammed as the prophet of God. No, I cannot do that. I have trusted him too long to desert him now. If need be I will sink with him to the bottom of hell."

But the conscience is quite as much against the preacher as is the old religious trust. Said a Persian to me, "When I hear you preach I feel that I must cease to lie and to steal and to do other sinful things. But I cannot afford to quit these sins. I cannot make a living in this country if I attempt to live as you teach us to live; so I do not like to hear about these things."—"But you," I said, "are a professed Christian, an Armenian; does not your own Bible teach you clearly what you must do?" —"Yes," he replied, "but my religion assures me that if I do commit these sins I can atone for them by giving the priest a karan or by fasting. But if I become a Protestant there is no alternative; I must quit my lying and cursing and stealing. I am not yet ready to do that. When I get to be rich enough to live honestly, then I will become a Protestant."

Under the power of these motives nearly every missionary's congregation disappears, in great part, after the first impulse of curiosity has ceased in the people. A very few persons, of all who came at first, may stand by him. One or two may believe; the multitude have deserted him. If now he resort to no other means of reaching and holding the people but his public preaching, what will he do for hearers? I know native Nestorian and Armenian preachers in the employ of the mission who at first had full houses, but who in a few weeks could muster no other hearers than the members of their own families. If the missionary will have a discussion with the priests or the mullahs, he can draw a crowd until the congregations are dispersed by a mob and a row or until the authorities interfere to prevent the mob. But the controversy, if possible at all, must soon end, and the missionary must rely on something more permanent and profitable. Many missionaries who have tried the public debate have had no hearers to show when the discussion had ceased. I have known also missionaries whose "polity" was to rely solely on preaching as the missionary agency, and who opposed schools and secular helps, who in time had no occasion to preach at all, solely because they could find no one to preach to. I have noticed that such persons are quite willing to preach to a congregation composed of the pupils of a school and their parents, however much they may be opposed on principle to mission-schools. A knowledge of the language of the country, fluency of speech, learning, and even deep piety and consecration, are of no avail to remedy the difficulty. It is as deeply seated as human depravity and as strongly intrenched as a false religion.

Under these conditions the missionary is depressed and mortified. He learns that method has something to do with successful fishing for men. He learns now, if he has not known it before this, that there is another kind of preaching and exposition of the gospel besides that of words. It is the preaching by acts of beneficence and by teaching and by social life. Satan is not all-wise and omnipresent; he cannot spend his strength at every point of approach. He has done his work thoroughly in the human heart on the strictly religious side of it; he has strongly fortified his position of defence there. Christ drew multitudes to his preaching by the hope of worldly gain of some sort. Not that he offered wealth or material gains. Quite the contrary. But he attracted the people by working miracles and by his very remarkable claims to Messiahship.

In Persia there are some persons who come to the missionary with sincere desire of knowing what he has to impart of religious knowledge. A few persons are moved with dissatisfaction with the prevalent religions. The great majority are swayed by considerations of some secular gain. Many persons are so desirous of having their children obtain the benefit of such secular knowledge as the missionaries can impart that they are willing to take the risk of Protestant influence over them. Some of them look forward to employment by Europeans for their children. Education is seen to be a great help. The influence gained with Persians by social intercourse is one that is unconsciously felt. By means of schools the attendance of the scholars on the services of public worship is secured. Here is given a permanent nucleus of a congregation. Social influences draw other persons, and the employees of the mission are required, if requirement be necessary, to attend the religious services. A permanent congregation and church are in time built up out of these elements, with an increasing power to draw to itself by means of the associations of its members. As the missionaries become known, opposition in time dies out or is futile. After the first struggles the natives gain confidence and venture more in connection with the work. Such is the usual course of growth to the missions in Persia. In no marked instance has there been a great turning of the people to Christ. The growth has been the result of patient toil continued year by year. The people of Eastern Persia have offered no great opportunities for gain by means of so-called revival labors. Public preaching for Mohammedans has been, as I have shown, in most places impracticable. The Christian communities where such effort might be possible are very few, and the people, except in the manner stated, have been disinclined to Protestant views. The Armenians are not gathered in large communities in this part of Persia. In truth, it may be said that the non-Mohammedans are not concentrated in large numbers in any part of the country. Jews have come in the way of our missionary work in Tehran, Hamadan and Mashhad only. The ingatherings of great revivals on mission-fields seem to come only after years of labor. The time since the beginning of the Eastern Mission has been the period of sowing and of preparation, the time of laying foundations and opening of highways. But these years have not been without important results. What these are has been shown in the course of this narrative.

It was thought to be desirable to employ native preachers and teachers as assistants of the missionaries in the opening of the mission. But great difficulty was experienced in obtaining the right kind of men for this service. At first it was wellnigh impossible to get a Nestorian preacher for either Tehran or Hamadan. There were two reasons for this: One was that few or none of the Nestorians are acquainted with the Persian or the Armenian language. They were, therefore, unable to labor efficiently with either the Mohammedans or the Armenians of Eastern Persia. All the Nestorians who at any time have attempted to preach in this section of the country have used the Turkish language, with which some of the people of this region have acquaintance. Another reason was the fact that Nestorians preferred, very naturally, to remain with their own people in Western Persia, there being none of this race in the eastern part. It was found to be impracticable to bring Armenian assistants from the Armenian communities of Turkey for many reasons: The work among their own people created a demand for nearly all who were prepared to preach; the very few who might be obtained had no knowledge of Persian; and the distance to be traveled by them to reach the field was so great as to make the change expensive and of very doubtful expediency. The only assistants available were the Armenians of Eastern Persia, and none of these had been trained in mission-schools or under our influence. They were unconverted men, but some of them were fairly well qualified by schools which they had attended, and they were specially fitted to do service by their knowledge of the Persian tongue and the Armenian language as spoken in this part of the land. Several Armenians were so employed, and all of them in time became members of the mission-churches.

The lack of qualified assistants made it necessary to organize a training-class of a few young men who should be prepared in the most essential things for serving as teachers, colporteurs and preachers. These persons have done fairly well; some of them have been efficient and valuable.

Congregations have been maintained permanently in several places in Tehran, Hamadan and Rasht, and part of the time in Karaghan. The work of preaching has been considered of first importance, and these congregations have been sustained by persevering and personal effort only. It is probable that they could not have been kept up without the schools which have been connected with them. The religious services in these congregations have been conducted, in the main, as similar services are in the home churches. It required no special training to enable the Persians to understand the proprieties of our public assemblies, for they have been accustomed to the public worship of the mosques and the Armenian churches. The forms of worship differ, but the people have been trained to habits of decorum and their manner is reverential. In no instance within my own knowledge has the congregation of a missionary been disturbed by any malicious or irreverent conduct. In this particular the Persians set an example which many of the people of Christian lands would do well to imitate. It should be said, however, that this orderly conduct is not the fruit of much liberty. It appears to be the fruit of rigid discipline. The people are accustomed to law and to obey, and are taught to respect their superiors in age and authority. Superstition also has something to do with their conduct in reference to religious exercises. Preaching is common to the public assemblies of the mosque at some seasons of the year. Persians, therefore, are not surprised to find preaching in mission-churches. It is less frequent in the Armenian congregations.

Music is unknown in Mohammedan worship. The intoning and chanting of Armenians can hardly be called musical. The public worship of mission-chapels is usually accompanied with singing and the harmonium. The music is not admired at first by Mohammedans; the impression made is not in accord with their notions of propriety and reverence. But this impression is soon effaced, and as soon as they can reconcile their conscience to it they listen with pleasure to Christian praise. Sacred song is a means of imparting religious impressions, and one which may be used in every place. It is not always of the best order, judged after an artistic standard, but the hearers are ignorant of the defects, and in a little while learn to join in the service. Native congregations seldom attain to any excellence in this exercise unless trained and led by the voice of a missionary. They invariably fall into the minor key, or that peculiar kind of singing common in that country, which is not much esteemed by themselves and is poorly adapted to the hymns commonly sung in the assemblies of Protestants. In nearly every mission-station the harmonium or reed-organ is used in the services of public worship, but I do not know that it or the singing serves to attract any persons to the congregation after the novelty of the first impression has ceased to be felt. The organ is useful, however, in leading the service of song. That part of the services in which Persians take most interest is the preaching. They judge of this by the usual standards of excellence, and they are most interested in the presentation of doctrines, and particularly those doctrines which touch their own faith and mode of worship. They consider the doctrine of a future life with special interest. The Christian presentation of Christ is in conflict with the teaching of the Koran. It is impossible to harmonize the two. The greatest differences are in the most important and essential points. The Mohammedan Persian makes no serious objection to any claim set up for Christ if we will omit the claim of his being the Son of God and the Redeemer. To claim divinity for a human being is no new thing to them. The Ale Allahees assert the divinity of Ale, the husband of Fatima, as their name denotes. This sect, though tolerated, is very greatly in the minority. The prevalent belief and preaching with reference to Ale is that he was a good man divinely called and inspired to preside over the destinies of Islam. But the Ale Allahees contend that he was God incarnate.

The peculiarities of the Persian Sheahism are not such that they call for any unusual methods of general missionary effort or in the presentation of the gospel. These peculiarities, however, do affect the Persian's relation to and apprehension of many of the methods and doctrines of Christianity. The Persians are almost wholly of the Mohammedan sect called the "Twelve." They differ from the Sunees, the larger division of Islam, not in the essential doctrines of theology, but in the principles and methods of the government of Islam. In these the Twelve appear to have borrowed from the New Testament and from Rome. The number of the twelve Imams might be reasonably conjectured to have been at first suggested by the twelve apostles. The claim to such prerogatives as are assumed for the Imams seems to have been taken from the claim for the apostles at first, and for the popes in a later age. The hint of the doctrine of the second coming of the Mahde might have been given by the doctrine of the second coming of Christ. Fatimism has some resemblance to Mariolatry. It might be thought, with show of reason, that Persians would be favorably inclined toward the papal Church because of these resemblances. But the fact appears to be that the peculiar doctrines and forms of worship of the Romish Church have no great weight with Sheahs. The two great sects of Islam have been in contact with

Rome nearly thirteen hundred years, and have received these marks of the beast, yet they manifest no tendency to yield to Rome. The Mohammedan revulsion from idolatry repels Persians as well as other Mohammedans from the papal Church. A reception of Christianity by them carries with it an abandonment of these resemblances. The force of an appeal to them in behalf of Christianity is broken by any attempt to ground it upon points of resemblance in it to their own system, except it be on such doctrines as are essential to any belief in the being and perfections of one supreme God. So far as Christianity resembles Islam, the former is thought to be unnecessary and a justification of the latter. It is the difference of the two systems which can affect Mohammedans with any concern. The gospel offers that which Sheahism has not: it offers a sacrifice for sin, salvation without works, and a God moved by love instead of one of justice only. This preaching is in conflict with Islam, but not offensively so. Missionary instruction cannot be confined to the statement of this prime feature of the gospel. Christianity is seen by many intelligent Persians to be in conflict with their philosophy, theology, ethics and forms of worship.

It is not necessary to change the method of preaching and form of truth in order to adaptation to the wants of Armenians. They are nearly as much in need of instruction in the evidences of Christianity and the subjects named above as the Mohammedans are, although they profess to be Christians. In labors of the missionaries for the Jews of Persia emphasis is put upon the proofs of the Messiahship of Jesus. This is the pivotal point of all labor with them. It is also an important point to gain with Mohammedans, for they believe that nearly all the Messianic prophecies relate to the office and authority of Mohammed. But little effort is made, however, to gain any of these people by direct assault on controverted points. The most successful means of prevailing with them is by a presentation of the spiritual condition of mankind and of the way of salvation by grace only. The truths which affect them most are presented in discussions in regard to which they have no answer—namely, the sinfulness of man, the perfection of the divine law, the failure of works and the sufficiency of Christ. The conviction of the unreasonableness and worthlessness of all attempts at justification by ceremonies carries with it an abandonment of all that is essentially Mohammedan.

The missionaries in Tehran have not received to the Church professed converts from any sect without a preparatory course of instruction. The schools give a good part of the training required in Bible knowledge. It is not possible for a pupil to be in these without obtaining some knowledge of the essential truths of the gospel. Converts not in the schools were expected to attend the religious services and to receive private instruction from the missionaries.

The course of study in the mission-schools has been from the first that of the common schools in Christian lands, with the addition of lessons from the Bible and from the Catechism. The Sabbath-schools are attended by the pupils of the day-schools and by members of the congregations. These and the weekly or daily prayer-meetings exhibit no marked differences from like meetings in Christian countries.

As will be seen by a perusal of the preceding pages of this work, this mission has given a great deal of care and labor to Bible-work within its own field. The fruits of this work are plainly apparent in every place where colporteurs have gone. The visible effects have been religious inquiry, an investigation of the claims of the Bible and a demand for books. The result with Armenians has been to supply them with Scriptures where they had none. In Tehran the circulation of the Scriptures has had the effect of silencing the opposition of some of the leading and most violent mujtaheeds. One, a man of great influence, was contemplating measures of opposition to the Tehran mission. He did not possess a copy of the Scriptures, and had not at any time of his life seen a copy of the Bible. A Christian Persian, hearing of the evil reports, called upon the mujtaheed and suggested that it would be much more to the credit of a judge to know from the book itself what Christians taught than to rely on the reports of ignorant and evil-disposed persons. The mujtaheed assented to this view of the matter, and requested the man to obtain a Bible for him, and that he should not let any one know of such request or that he had the book in his possession. On reading the volume he expressed his surprise, and nothing further was ever heard of the resentment of this mujtaheed. In several instances known to me the gift of a Bible and the perusal of it by Persian officers have been the direct means of leading these men to protect the colporteurs and Christians and to open the way for our work. With reference to the circulation of other books little can be said, because there are very few Christian books in the Persian language. The mission has made no attempt to distribute the controversial works of Pfander. However good, therefore, the book may be, no claim is made by us for the use of it except as a text-book for the training-class. The work is useful to Persian students in our schools as a presentation of the Mohammedan controversy, but its general circulation is prohibited. The school and religious books in the Armenian language are useful in their place, but the religious books are chiefly translations of works composed in the English language and adapted to Western ideas and customs of life, and to a maturity of Christian knowledge which is not possessed by Armenians in any considerable degree, and not at all by Mohammedans. Our work in Tehran and Eastern Persia has need of books written in adaptation to Persian modes of life and thought, and made attractive by simplicity, also by illustrations. The Persians are very fond of pictures: they love to paper the walls of their houses with Harper's and Frank Leslie's illustrated papers, and in efforts to meet their wants in the way of books it is poor economy to leave the illustrations out and to fill up with dry dissertations. The popular editions of their own books abound in illuminations.

The Eastern Persia Mission makes use of the medical missionary. Among the friends of missions there is a growing interest in the medical mission. It is thought to be desirable, not only for the safety of the families of missionaries, but as a means of influence over natives of the country. The physician gains access to Persians over whom the clerical missionary could obtain but little or no influence, and this for two reasons: first, because of the medical treatment he can give; and, secondly, for the reason that he is supposed not to be a religious teacher. So far as my own observation of medical work in Persia extends, it goes to prove that just so far as the physician makes direct religious effort for his patients or the people at large he is avoided by all who shun any other missionary. I have not seen any considerable or permanent increase of the congregations from the dispensary. The effect of preaching in the dispensary has been to lessen the number of those who resort to that place. As soon as the impression is created that the dispensary is a net in which to catch proselytes or hearers for the congregation, the medical department loses the patronage of the better classes of the people. The real efficiency of the medical mission has been in the indirect influence exerted by the formation of friendships with all classes, and especially with the authorities. The effect is not seen in great religious gain, but in a secular advantage. The conferring of medals and honors by the king on our physicians is not to be taken as any indication of the conversion of the Shah to Christianity. It is encouraging, however, to learn that he is more and more favorably inclined to Christian therapeutics. The chief benefit of the medical mission, so far as one can judge, is in the preservation of the health and life of the men and women whose whole business it is to make direct religious effort for the natives. The medical department in Tehran is yet new, and that in Hamadan is more recent. The establishment in Tehran of the hospital which is now in process of construction will, it is believed, give the doctor greater opportunity than is at present offered for direct religious labors with the people.

Special effort for the religious improvement of Persian women has been made mainly in or by the girls' schools. Reports of efforts made for women outside of the schools have been given in these pages. The want of help for this department will in part be supplied by the presence of a lady physician. The social life of Persian women is such that Christ can be preached to them in Persian homes most effectually by Christian women only.

CHAPTER XII.

Difficulties Peculiar to the Field—Expensive Establishments—Display of Wealth—Educational Establishments—Similarity of Motives in Tehran and in New York—Missionaries are Representatives—Impression Created by Foreign Legations—Criticism of Missionaries—Requirements in the Way of Schools—Judicious Use of Funds—Espionage of the Persian Authorities—Preoccupation of the Minds of the People by Worldly Allurements—Usual Influence of Foreigners—Demand for Foreign Protection—Advantages of the Field—A Centre of Influence for the Kingdom—Political Influences—Persian Young Men—Good Influence of Foreigners—Consecration of Wealth.

EVERY missionary field has its own peculiar difficulties in the way of mission-work. Tehran is no exception in this particular. One of the most obvious demands of the place is an expensive establishment. Being, as it is, the capital of the kingdom and residence of the king, his court and many wealthy and influential men, the citizens of the place have been accustomed to the style of living maintained by such persons. Not that they all live as princes—far from it—but the poorest of the people are familiar with the show and luxury of the great. They look with deference upon palaces, parks and royal equipages, and the environments of the representatives of courts and princes are, in their minds, associated with respectability and with efficiency in every undertaking of a public nature. Here, as in no other city of the kingdom, poverty and the want of a fair worldly estate are a source of weakness. The people have sense and discrimination enough to know that the religious orders are not expected to live as princes, yet impressions are made upon their minds of the same nature and to the same extent as those which are created by the environments of every Church and religious enterprise in America or in England. Influence must be gained mainly by the established channels. The people are not like the naked savages of Africa and the islands, but a cultivated people whose taste and sense of propriety are formed in a centre of Oriental splendor, and it is not to be presumed that they will be ready to receive shabby representatives of Christian zeal. If the missionary could command the power by which the apostles and the Saviour himself proved their divine mission—the power of working miracles, of curing the sick by a word and raising the dead—he might be expected to have a following; but in the absence of these accessories he is judged by precisely the same criterions by which people in Christian lands judge of men and their undertakings.

There is in Tehran not only a display of wealth in the secular life of all classes, but in the religious and educational establishments as well. These are on a scale with the pretensions of the ambitious classes. There are many large mosques with fair appointments and revenues. The number of such is increasing. One mosque is estimated to cost over two millions of dollars. The mujtaheeds and Mohammedan preachers are among the best educated and cultured of the people. I do not now compare these men and their establishments with like institutions and orders of men in Europe and America, but they are notable in their own country, and missionaries could not expect to rival these institutions in point of expensiveness. But on this point it is plain too great a contrast would naturally excite contempt.

It may be said that the people's habits of thought and feeling in regard to these matters should form no criterion of conduct for the missionaries, and that they should not think of commending their cause by conformity to the worldly and ostentatious ways of the heathen. The same arguments for conformity to public taste which are urged in the appointments of churches and schools in America are, within reasonable limits, valid in Persia and in every other mission-field. The dirty and poor chapels of New York or London are not the places to which the masses resort, much less the respectable classes. The schools and colleges in America which have not adequate means of support are not the schools which are most patronized. The feelings of many Americans and Englishmen toward rude appointments in churches and schools are evidences of the sentiments which are cherished by all people of any refinement of feeling, whether in Persia or in other civilized lands. Missionaries, however pure their doctrine, cannot afford to disregard and shock the taste and sense of propriety of the civilization under which the people are reared. These feelings are deepened in Persians by the belief that Christian missionaries have a constituency possessed of great wealth, and that if there be any lack of adequate equipment it is either because the missionary is not approved or because that constituency do not esteem his work.

The life of the representatives of European governments confirms this impression of the natives. The legations are maintained at what seems to this people a great expense. The buildings occupied by them are spacious and the best which the country affords. They support many servants, and command the respect of the king and his courtiers by their style of living, if not by other means. While it is not expected that missionaries will be maintained in the same style of luxury, yet it is thought that they also are in no small degree representatives of the life and civilization of Christian nations. I am sure there is no desire on the part of missionaries to emulate the manner of life of courtiers. But it is evident that in such a place the appointments for work must be of a very different grade from those which would be available in some other towns. The chapels must be fair structures. The mission-schools must be superior to the best schools conducted by Mohammedans and Armenians. There must be superiority in the ar-

British Legation.

Page 305.

rangement and the instruction of these schools. In view of these facts, some missionaries might prefer other fields and places in which this difficulty is not to be met, and where they will be free from all criticisms on the subject. It may be said, however, that when once the field has been possessed, the foundation laid and the buildings erected, the critics are among the most forward to occupy and to contribute their quota to the increase of expenses. The difficulty referred to was one which appeared at the first thought of occupying Tehran, and was seriously urged against any attempt to establish a mission-station there. But the same arguments might be presented in opposition to the opening of missions in any capital or in the great cities of other countries.

The question, "What is a judicious use of missionary funds to meet the proper demands of the place?" has been one of the most serious and perplexing questions which the missionaries in Tehran have had to consider. The limited allowances made by the Board have left but little or no room for doubt in practice.

Another source of embarrassment peculiar to this field is the fact that missionary work in the capital falls immediately under the observation of the king and the highest secular and religious authorities of that country. It might reasonably be expected that this work would excite the jealousy of the latter and the opposition of both, to some extent. But the fact is, that no great difficulty has arisen from this source, other than such as is met with in other parts of Persia. It appears to be true that the mission here has suffered less restraint than missions in other cities. It is possible that the future may show that the conjectured evil has a foundation in fact. The future must depend upon the character of the men who may rule in the high places of the government. The danger furnishes a motive for special prayer that He who turneth the king's heart whithersoever he will may incline the king of Persia to favor the cause of the ministers of Christ.

The preoccupation of the minds of the people of Tehran by objects of an enticing and worldly nature is thought to be a condition unfavorable to the development of religious and spiritual feeling and instruction among the people of Tehran. Some of these objects have been referred to in connection with other subjects. We have here the glare and pomp of Oriental state. The king and his court form a conspicuous object in the eyes of the people, and the manner of life of the principal men tends to the development of the natural love of the world and special forms of its vanities. Many of the men in authority are openly intemperate, while the use of intoxicating drinks in the greater part of the country is not tolerated by Mohammedans. Many of the people are extravagant in their dress and style of living, and the tendency with the populace is to follow the example of the wealthy. The poor and the people of moderate means are constantly tempted to live beyond their ability.

The presence of men of wealth at the capital often stimulates trade and speculation and increases the covetousness so proverbially strong in Orientals. It also engages the thoughts of business-men, so that they are less inclined to religious services than are the people in many other places. The Persians of Tehran have learned some of the tricks of speculation. They know what it is to make a "corner" in wheat and other things. They have learned to speculate in city property and play sharp in making advances in the price of corner lots. They have learned how to build to sell, and to sell in more ways than one. Some of the merchants have visited European cities, and regularly purchase stocks of goods in London, Paris, Vienna and Moscow.

Public affairs also often offer exciting phases. The removal from office of favorites of the court or of the people, and the appointment of other men to fill the places vacated, the rumors of revolt or war, the arrival or departure of the ministers of foreign governments, new orders of the Shah, the movements of troops and many other incidents, all furnish occasion for gossip and for suspicion where rumor is the only source of information to the populace.

The usual influence of foreigners is thought to be adverse to Christian effort with the natives of the country. With a few noble exceptions the foreigners are not examples of Christian character. On the contrary, some of them are conspicuous for immorality and intemperance.

The natives imitate the vices rather than the virtues of foreigners. Not the least of the evils to be met in the course of mission-work in the capital is the demand for foreign protection on the part of Persians who become in any way identified with missionaries or other foreigners. This trouble is felt in every part of Persia where foreigners reside. All the people experience such grievances that they resort to foreigners in the hope that relief will be obtained through their intercessions with the Persian authorities. This hope is increased by the evidence of influence seen in the foreign legations. It is often the case that Persians seek the friendship of missionaries in the expectation of this temporal advantage when they should be actuated by better motives. No man of kind feeling and having real sympathy with the people in their distresses would refuse to aid when assistance could possibly be given. His natural impulse is to intercede for the oppressed. The customs of the country are such that he can often render efficient service in this way. The right of the teacher to intercede for his disciples, the master for his servants, appears to be conceded by the authorities, and is so common a practice that he who should disregard the privilege could hardly retain the affection or respect of those who look to him for instruction. Much of the missionary's time, therefore, is taken up with a consideration of, or an effort to relieve, the distresses of the people for whom he ministers.

We turn from the consideration of the difficulties to

a view of the advantages of the position. The capital of Persia is the centre of the influences which affect the whole kingdom for either good or evil. It is true of nearly all Oriental countries that the residence of the king and the seat of government make the chief city. The population follows the person of the king. It certainly has been true of Persia in all past time that the permanent seat of the court has been the principal city in every way. Here are concentrated the political influences, the educational institutions, such as they may be, the literary men and the military leaders. Here, as in no other place, missionary influence might be expected to reach the governing classes. Some obscure village or provincial capital may bring the missionary into intimate relations with some man who in the providence of God may be raised to the highest place in the government, but under ordinary providences acquaintance with the rulers and influence with them are obtained at the capital city. While Protestant missionaries do not advise schemes of political influence, yet the friendship of the rulers of the land is to be desired so far as it may be honestly obtained.

It is a fact worthy of note that from the capital of Persia many young men go out to different parts of the land to serve the state in many ways, as in the army, in the postal and telegraphic departments and as physicians. It is not unreasonable to believe that some or many of these persons during their life in the city may come under the influence of the gospel, and carry that influence with them to many positions of power in other parts of the country. Several young men might be named who have been associated in some way with the missionaries of Tehran and have received appointments to responsible positions remote from the capital. One, a member of the Tehran church, has for years been in the service of the king in one of the principal towns of North-western Persia and on the borders of the Turkman country; another is near the eastern frontier; another was appointed to Hamadan. In no other city in the kingdom is there an opening of the same extent for the employment of Christian young men in positions of influence under the government of that country, and where they are yet free to exercise their own religious convictions. It should not be supposed that the only persons sent out from the capital on the service of the king are young men from the schools. The missionary in that city is known personally or by report to nearly all the heads of the departments of state and to the greater part of the subordinate officers. Many of these from time to time go with the army or in other service to different parts of the country, and others come to take their places.

In no other city of the kingdom are there so many readers. This fact shows the possibility of accomplishing much good in this city by the circulation of Christian books. It is probably true also that in no other city of that land are there so many literary men, and therefore there is no other place where there is so fair a prospect of accessions to our number from this class of men. If it be thought that their literature and education are of no value, it must nevertheless be admitted that they are believed by the people to possess worth. It is also true that these men are the leaders of the people, and especially influential with the better class of citizens. The knowledge which they possess is an important qualification for dealing with the errors which the literature and education serve to perpetuate.

If the presence of foreigners has its evils, it also has its advantages. Many of them are well disposed to the missionaries, some of them are earnest Christian men and women, and nearly all are kindly disposed to Christian effort. Owing to the isolation of foreigners in Persia, they and the missionaries are brought into intimate and friendly relations, and are to some extent mutually dependent. It is possible that much good may be done by cultivating this friendship and directing the exercise of the influence which the foreigners, especially the English-speaking people, possess. The mission-work gives to all among them who may be kindly disposed a favorable opportunity of aiding the cause of Christ and of benefiting the native population.

If there is at the capital a concentration of wealth, and if this may increase the power of a false religion, yet we may trust that the gospel has power to bring these possessions also into subserviency to its own good purpose. We may believe that this wealth and the glory of the kingdom will one day be consecrated to Christ.

CHAPTER XIII.

Difficulties and Encouragements in the Whole Field—Intolerance—Peculiarities of Persian Mohammedanism—The Weaker Phase—The Difficulty of the Mental Condition—Policy of European Governments—Dispersed State of the Non-Mohammedan People—Encouragements—Increase of Intelligence, Means of: Telegraphs, Postal System—Favorable Impression of Foreigners—Results of Missionary Work—Precedents in Favor of Religious Liberty—Success of Bible-Work—Exploration—Preparatory Work—Present and Prospective Effect of the Russian Advance on the Eastern Border of Persia—Natural Resources of Eastern Persia—Elements of Change—Policy of European Nations.

THE statements of the foregoing chapter have special reference to Tehran. But there are difficulties and advantages experienced in the missionary work which pertain to the whole field of Eastern Persia.

It will be seen from the course of the government and the experiences of the missionaries, as related in previous chapters, that the great obstacle to mission efforts in Persia is the intolerance of the secular and spiritual authorities. It is so in the whole land. But, as might be expected, that intolerance is intense and effective in proportion to the strength and pride of the people. Evangelical labors in this field have to do with Armenians, Jews and Mohammedans only or mainly. There are many Jewish and Armenian communities in which the people fear to receive the labors of Christian missionaries, not because of intolerant laws of the secular government, but from fear of the opposition and persecution which would be excited against them by the leaders of these sects, and which could not be immediately suppressed owing to the indifference of the secular authorities to matters of this sort.

How far the peculiar religious faith of Persian Mohammedans may form a discouraging element to be met with is a question which has not been fairly answered by labors for Persians, owing to the fact that intolerant laws have so far precluded such labors that the real strength of the system of philosophy and religion has not been tested. From what has been done, and judging of the theory, it seems to be a fair inference that the system has no great inherent strength and no great or peculiar element of influence as against other systems of religion. It appears to be the weaker phase of Mohammedanism. The extravagances and the unnatural phases of the system are elements of weakness. The claim made by the Mahde is received with reservations and skepticism by the people. There is an element of absurdity in the serious pretensions set up for him by the history and traditions of the Twelve. This doctrine is an element of weakness also by reason of the dissensions which it creates. It gives rise to divisions about his powers, and gives occasion to an interminable succession of impostors. The main conception of the succession of twelve Imams is so palpable an imitation of the number and power of twelve apostles that the resemblance suggests to every intelligent person the thought of an invention and a fraud. The system, however, presents the difficulty there is in the condition of the intellect and heart which can accept it. It might be expected that the only way of leading such a mind to receive another and better system would be to instruct and enlighten it. We believe that the main reason that so few Mohammedans have become Christians is the fact that the knowledge and education essential to a preparation for the reception of Christianity have been excluded by the intolerance which owes much of its efficiency to European diplomacy. European governments have discouraged all effort on the part of their subjects for the Persian people. This discouragement has included commercial as well as religious efforts. It has taken the form of positive prohibition to live in the country or to enter into any contracts with the government or people of that kingdom. This policy has been adopted as a safeguard against any political complications. For this purpose the scheme may or may not be wise, but, however that may be, it has tended to the exclusion of the gospel from this and other Mohammedan lands.

The dispersed condition of the non-Mohammedan people has its favorable and unfavorable bearing on missionary effort. The settlements of the Armenians, Jews and Guebers are widely separated and are feeble. This condition exposes these people to the influence of the Mohammedans among whom they are dispersed; it also makes missionary effort for them more laborious than it would be were these colonies concentrated in one. The Protestant communities are necessarily small. On the other hand, this state may be thought to have its advantages. It gives opportunity for many centres of Christian influences among the Mohammedans. Every Armenian and Jewish colony when once evangelized becomes a light to a wide region where now the gospel is practically excluded.

We now turn our thoughts to the encouragements offered to missionary labor.

It is a fact of no little interest that there is an increase of intelligence in the people of Eastern Persia. There are special reasons why it is so. Within a few years past these people have been brought, as never before, into communication with the world and into contact with Christian civilization. Special means of awakening inquiry and diffusing knowledge have been established in the land. Of these means mention may be made of the telegraph-lines constructed by Europeans. The stations along these lines are in the hands of operators who have been especially instructed and who are inclined to progress. An efficient postal system has been established. It gives communication with all the provinces and principal towns and with Europe and America. Many of the postmasters are Armenians, and all have had some instruction. The telegraph and the post speak for progress and for the Christian nations. The king's college sends out a number of physicians having some knowledge of medical science as it is taught by Europeans. The inclination of the people is favorable to foreigners. A foreigner of good deportment is usually treated with great respect. He is considered superior to the native Persian, and his superiority speaks favorably for his religious faith or the faith of his people. It is commonly remarked by Persians that the best religion is that which is accepted by the best and wisest nation. They think that Persians are the best and wisest, or that Mohammedans are, until they see that the superiority is with other people.

The results of missionary work in Eastern Persia promise well for the future. This work, as the foregoing narrative shows, is of recent date. It began with a single mission-station; it has expanded to several stations. It began with one missionary; it now employs eleven and a goodly number of native teachers and assistants, and calls for more laborers to meet the demands of the growing interest and the opening fields. This mission has had success in several clearly-defined lines of effort. Which one of these may be the most important in its bearing upon the interests of the whole field I would not attempt to decide; but in referring to them I would mention—

First, the gain in precedents in favor of religious liberty and other concessions on the part of the Persian authorities. In the early days of missionary effort in Persia control over the belief and worship of the people of a religious sect was referred by the secular ruler to the spiritual head of that sect. The bishop, and after him the priests, of the Armenians claimed the right to judge of all departures from Armenian faith and practice on the part of the people, and the right to inflict penalties, to restrain, imprison and to punish all who felt constrained to adopt another belief and form of worship. Like authority was exercised by the heads of other non-Mohammedan sects. It was needful, therefore, that the missionary should find some way of protecting converts to his views of religious truth. He could protect the convert only by securing the interposition of the secular authorities. That interposition was dependent on the caprice of the prince, governor or king. The decisions of the judge were sometimes favorable to the appeal of the missionary, and often adverse. In the course of the years of the mission's continuance some general orders of the authorities in Tehran have been obtained declaring the religious liberty of all non-Mohammedans; but the most effectual helps are the decisions in particular cases, which may be referred to as precedents establishing important principles by which the relations of the sects are to be regulated. In many cases also where no judicial action was called for, in matters of title to property, relations of missionaries to the sects, duties of converts to the state and questions of privilege, the authorities in Tehran have made important concessions.

Secondly, the general circulation of the Scriptures in Persia, especially in Eastern Persia. A special effort in this direction has been continued during the years of this mission. Previous to the opening of the Tehran mission efforts for a general distribution of the Bible were spasmodic and after long intervals of time. In fact, we think there was no attempt made to penetrate to the villages and secluded districts remote from the great thoroughfares. The circulation of the Scriptures in the Persian language was thought to be extremely dangerous, and possibly impracticable, in other places than the great cities or among Armenians and non-Mohammedans. Colporteurs from Tehran have traversed every province and district in Central and Eastern Persia as far south as Ispahan and Yezd and as far east as Merv in Turkistan and Herat in Afghanistan. The development of the Bible-work by the Tehran mission presented such encouragement to increased exertion in this line of Christian work that the British and Foreign Bible Society was led to enter the field and to establish an agency for Southern Persia, while at the same time the American Bible Society sent out an agent to supervise and extend the work in Northern Persia. The great extent to which the Scriptures in Persian and Turkish have been circulated is itself a result worthy of all the effort made for it, and is so much direct missionary labor for Mohammedans. The distribution of the Bible is an efficient means now available for letting in the light on Mohammedans, who are supposed to be so inaccessible. It is sincerely to be hoped that the advantage gained by the two Bible societies will be duly appreciated, and that their occupation of the country will not be in name merely, and that they will not doze over their possessions. I believe that Mr. Whipple, the agent of the American Bible Society, has endeavored to hold the positions gained in all his broad field, extending from the Arras to the Tejend River and from Ararat to the Domine Kuh.

Thirdly, the work of exploration. The missionaries of Tehran have personally become acquainted with the principal places in all the provinces of the central and north-eastern regions. From the capital they have traveled westward to Tabriz and Hamadan and northward to Gelan and Mazandaran, southward to Ispahan and east to Mashhad. It is some indication of the absence of such exploration in this field to say that we have no evidence of the visit of any foreign missionary to the Armenian settlement of Karaghan and to Mashhad until these places were visited by a missionary of Tehran, except the journey of Joseph Wolff to the latter place early in this century and while on his way to Bokhara. This we say with no purpose of boasting, but with a view to show the condition of the missionary work. A knowledge of the field is a desirable attainment as a preparation for the most practicable direction of labor. This work has called for extended tours which, though in some instances made with haste, yet resulted in much religious and Christian effort in places both near to and remote from Tehran. Besides these specialties, much has been accomplished in the usual lines of missionary work—namely, by preaching, by schools and by the organization of churches. The last-named work implies the conversion of souls. An extended preparatory work has been done. Important results have been attained, but there must be, we believe, an unseen influence proceeding from the labors of foreign and native missionaries, from preaching, teaching, books and social intercourse with the people, far greater in future results than any fruits now visible.

In speaking of the encouraging attainments and prospects we ought to mention the present and prospective effect on Eastern Persia of the Russian advance on the eastern border. The insecurity of those regions prevented the improvement of that country, and made that part of the land one of the most unpromising. But now a railway is completed along the border to the confines of Afghanistan, which makes that section the most available part of the country from the Caspian Sea. The friends of peace and civilization must hail that advance with pleasure as a promise of better times for the people of those long-desolated regions. The railway destined to unite the Indus and the Caspian Sea skirts the eastern frontier, and is completed for more than half that distance, and trains of cars are running to the Afghan line. It may be predicted that the same interests which make telegraphs from the Black Sea to the Persian Gulf necessary will also make railways essential along the southern base of the Elburz Mountains to the Caucasus and the Black Sea, if not in other directions. The railway and telegraph are efficient agents in dispersing the ignorance and superstition in which the religions of the Old World find their security. Their advent is to be greeted as the forerunner of a higher civilization and of Christianity in that land.

Persia is a land of deserts, and is known in the present time for the poverty of her people and for the charm which the history and romance of the past have thrown about her name. But she really needs only the moral elements of advancement to attain a place of eminence among the nations. She possesses very many sources of wealth. Her deserts need only the supply of water, which seems to be available, in order to make them verdant meadows and fruitful fields. Her forests abound in valuable and rare timber. Her mountains conceal rich ores and precious stones. Her climate surpasses that of every other Asiatic country in salubrity. The variety of the productions of the soil is very great. Her people are healthful, athletic and frugal, of sprightly intellect, strongly emotional, amiable and poetical nature. They are susceptible of culture in a marked degree. Confident in the sources of renovation for this land, we may look forward to a new Persia to arise out of the old and prepared to utilize the elements of greatness possessed by her. To one looking now on that country as it is, the realization of this expectation may seem to be very far in the future; but the elements of change have been fairly introduced, and as they have never been before. The pressure from without upon the old institutions of the country is increasing. The future of Persia is to be determined almost wholly by the policy of European nations. Her destiny seems to be in the power of England and Russia. Mutual jealousies on their part may lengthen the reign of the present order of things in that land. On the contrary, by timely encouragement of good tendencies and Christian influences they may soon see Persia in the ranks of the progressive nations of the world.

CHAPTER XIV.

Providential Calls—Power of Social Influences—Plea for some Isolated Communities—Abasabad Georgians—Jews of Mashhad—A College in Tehran, Reasons for.

THERE are some marked openings and providential calls for Christian effort in Eastern Persia. The common means of evangelization will be used: there is hardly any limit to the possibility of success in the use of such means. The conversion of the people must be effected, if at all, by the teaching of the Bible by the missionary. But Christianity is commended to men for their acceptance by other things than the written word. Christ is preached by example and by charity as well as by the word. Reverence for the Bible and our dependence upon formal acts of religious worship too often may be substituted for that social life and converse, and that active effort to relieve the necessities of mankind, which in Christ's life seemed to be as effectual as his word.

In missionary work among Mohammedans more might be done by social life. Public and formal teaching may not, at present, be practicable with them to any great extent, but there seems to be no barrier to friendly intercourse with the people. Rigorous as the law of apostasy from Islam may be, and while it may prevent the public, formal gathering of the people for worship, yet there is nothing in it to prevent friendly intercourse with Persians. This kind of labor will be most practicable for native Christians, and will naturally become more efficient and available as the number of qualified assistants is increased and as the missionaries find time for tours in the cities and villages of the secluded districts, where Europeans are unknown, and as they follow up the opportunities given in places where they have previously been or those in which the way for them has been prepared by native helpers.

A special plea might be made in behalf of certain isolated communities of nominal Christians in Eastern Persia, such as that at Abasabad in Khorasan, and referred to on a previous page. Missionary effort could be of little avail to such people so long as they remain in their present position. Having been forced to become Mohammedans, at least nominally, they must be put in some place of greater security than that which they now occupy before missionary effort could be made with any reasonable prospect of success. Their removal is entirely practicable, and should be effected at once. But it can be done only by the intervention in their behalf of foreign influence. The colony is not large, and therefore the removal is practicable. It might be thought that this change should be effected by themselves, but the suggestion is quite unreasonable. They now have certain rights and revenues secured by firman of the shahs which they would lose were they to remove without the consent of the king. Being Georgians, there is no Christian sect with which they could affiliate except it be with Protestants. Having once been recognized as Mohammedans, it would be unsafe for them to be known now as Christians unless they were protected by the government or were removed to a place where their change of faith would either be unknown or would excite no opposition. It should be remembered that they know of no affiliations except with the people of their own colony and race. It is unchristian to leave them so helpless under the power of Mohammedans. They should be taught the way to change their condition, and should be objects of special care, as they are subject to special evils.

There are other small colonies in like condition, both of Georgians and Jews. Special missionary effort in behalf of such colonies with a view to the improvement of their condition in material as well as spiritual matters is called for, and would be productive of good results and be justified by the Church at home. The writer earnestly hopes and prays that Christian men and women of means may be led to consider the deplorable state of these remnants of Christ's flock, and be constrained to aid in their deliverance. The sum of ten thousand dollars judiciously expended would be sufficient to remove this Georgian colony to or near the capital, and provide them with all necessary means in the way of homes and schools. The Jewish colony in Mashhad ought to have been removed long since. No Jewish or Armenian settlement would ever be made in that city by the choice of these people; they were carried thither by order of one of the shahs, and have been captives in that city. It may be said that all the non-Mohammedans are captives in Persia. The greater part of these people have long since ceased to be captives in fact, but some of the colonies remain virtually such to this time. It is to the latter that these remarks have special reference.

Not the least among the opportunities of benefiting the people of Persia is the opening in Tehran for a first-class college like Roberts College at Constantinople or the American institution at Beyrout. The founding of such institutions seems to be the order of the day on mission-fields. The fact is evidence of a demand and a reason for them. The reasons which justify the use of large sums of money for such schools in other countries are all in force in Tehran. The college at Oroomiah, though efficient and desirable, cannot meet the requirements of the whole kingdom in the way of educational advantages, and does not assume to do so. It must necessarily receive its patronage in the way of pupils from the Nestorians or from Western Persia, to whose wants it will be especially adapted by location and by the language used. If such a school may be expected to be useful in any mission-field, such expectation may be formed of one opened in the capital of Persia. There it will have the widest influence possible in that land. It will reach the largest number of the people and the most influential classes. It would necessarily offer special inducements to non-Mohammedans. The Shah has a college in Tehran which is attended by youth from all the religious sects and races, but Christian and Jewish youth, as well as Mohammedan, are obligated to some Mohammedan observances, and no direct Christian influences can here find a place, for the management is distinctly Mohammedan, though not officiously so. It is a pity that Christian youth should be left to such influences. It is impossible to send them all to European schools. The people are too poor and unlettered to provide for their own wants or to meet their own wishes in this particular. Their poverty will compel them to accept Mohammedan schools so far as these meet their wants. The people most eager for educational advantages are the non-Mohammedans. Men who have wealth to consecrate to a good purpose will find in the round of the mission-fields no country more destitute of Christian enterprise than Persia, and no sphere or place of educational work more promising than the capital of the Shah.

CHAPTER XV.

The Bible in Persia—No Evidence of Christian Literature in Persian in Early Times—The Bible First in Importance—First Version of any Part of the Bible in Persian—Version of Tus—Version of Kaffa—Version of Wheeloc and Pierson—Earlier Conjectured Version—Version of Nadir Shah—Version of Col. Colbrook—Version of L. Sebastiani—Version of Henry Martyn—Version of the Psalter by Henry Martyn—Dates of Publication of Different Editions—Glen's Version of the Psalms—Poetical and Prophetical Books—Version of the Historical Books by Pinkerton and Lee—Publication of Glen's Version of the Psalms and Proverbs—Glen's Version of the Old Testament, printed at Edinburgh—Robinson's Version of the Old Testament—Version of the Psalms by Mirza Abraham—Calcutta Edition of Martyn's Version—Lithograph Edition of Robinson's Version—Bruce's Version—Versions in Turkish—Amirchanjanz's Version in Transcaucasian Tartar—Publication of the Transcaucasian Version—Labaree's Version in Azarbijanee—Bassett's Version in Turkmanee—Difficulties in the Way of Translating in Persian—Great Size of the Volume of the Persian Bible—New Edition in Small Size—Lodiana Edition—Efforts in the Way of the Circulation of the Scriptures in Persia—Favorable Attitude of the Persian Government toward Christian Literature—Other Religious Books in Persian—By Whom and When Made—Books in Persian Turkish.

THE Persian language and literature bear no evidence of the presence in former ages of a Christian literature in the Persian tongue. It is reasonable to believe that if there had been any, some record of it would have remained or marked traces of its influence would have been seen in Persian books, but neither evidence is found.

Of modern evangelical agencies in Persia, the first in importance is the Scriptures in the languages spoken in that country, especially the Persian tongue. Other books are important aids to the missionary, but he will be greatly hindered without the Scriptures in the vernacular. Though translations of parts of the Bible into the Persian were made many centuries ago, the general circulation of the book has here, as in other places, awaited the efforts of the Bible and missionary societies.

The first version of any part of the Bible into Persian was a translation of the Pentateuch by Jacob, a Jewish rabbi of the city of Tus in Khorasan. The date of the translation is unknown, but it is thought that it cannot be earlier than the eighth or later than the tenth century. This version was first printed in Constantinople in 1546 with the Hebrew text, the Chaldee Targum of Onkelos and the Arabic version of Sudias Gaon.

Abaka of the Moghul dynasty died in A. D. 1282. He is supposed to have been a Christian. Soon after his death the Gospels were translated into Persian. A Persian manuscript version of the four Gospels was in the possession of Dr. Pocock, and was dated A. D. 1314. It was said to have been first printed in the London Polyglot by Bishop Walton.

It is stated also that a version of the four Gospels is printed in the London Polyglot which is conjectured to have been written at Kaffa, a town of the Krimea, by a Roman Catholic, and in A. D. 1341. It is believed to have been made from the Peshito Syriac.

A version of the Gospels was begun by Wheeloc, professor of Arabic in Cambridge, and after his death was completed by Pierson and published in 1657. The editors of this version are said to have used the same manuscript as that from which the version in the London Polyglot was printed. They are supposed also to have possessed two other manuscripts.

It is conjectured that there was a much older version of the Gospels, which De Long thinks was translated in 1388, and sent by Jerome Xavier, a Jesuit, from Agra to the College Romanum.

The next effort to make a version of the Scriptures into Persian was that of Nadir Shah. With reference to this Hanway appears to be the principal source of information. He says, in substance, that toward the close of A. D. 1740, Nadir Shah caused a translation of the four Gospels to be made into Persian. The work was placed under the supervision of his secretary, Mirza Mahde, a noted writer and scholar. He, being empowered for this purpose, "summoned several Armenian bishops and priests, together with divers missionaries of the Romish Church and Persian mullahs, to meet him at Ispahan. Many of the latter gave bribes in order to escape the task. "Among the Christians summoned on this occasion, only one Romish priest born in Persia was sufficient master of the language to enter upon a work of so critical a nature." " As to the Armenians, though they are born subjects of Persia and intermixed with the inhabitants, yet there are very few of them who understand the language fundamentally." This translation was dressed up with all the glosses which the fables and perplexities of the Koran could warrant. "Their chief guide was an ancient Arabic and Persian translation." Father de Vignes, a French missionary, was also employed in this work, in which he made use of the Vulgate edition. "The translators were but six months in completing this translation and transcribing several fair copies of it." In May, A. D. 1741, the work was presented to Nadir, then encamped with his court near Tehran. In this interview the Shah ridiculed some parts, and also ridiculed the Jews, also Mohammed and Ale alike. He remarked that the evangelists did not agree, " therefore he must remain under the same difficulty that he was under before;" that out of (both), if it pleased God to give him health, he would engage to make a religion much better than any which had yet been practiced by mankind.

We are told that as the style in which the gospel of the Polyglot is written has long been antiquated in Ispahan, several efforts have been made during the present century to produce a version in the polished dialect now spoken by the Persians. A translation of the four Gospels was made under the direction of Col. Colbrook, and published at Calcutta in 1804, but appears not to have been extensively circulated. Rev. L. Sebastiani completed a translation of the New Testament to near the end of the Epistles in the year 1812. A thousand copies of the Gospels of this version were printed at Serampore in the same year. This version is said to have been designed for the use of the Christians in Persia. Sebastiani had resided at the court of Persia. Sabat and Mirza Fitrut were employed by Henry Martyn to translate the whole of the New Testament. These men had been previously employed as translators, the one at Serampore and the other by Col. Colbrook. This translation was completed in 1808. But as it was thought to abound too much in Arabic terms, Henry Martyn decided to visit Persia for the purpose of effecting a revision in more idiomatic Persian. He entered Shiraz in 1811, and remained there nearly a year. Having completed the revision, he returned toward England, passing through Tehran and Tabriz, but died at Tokat in Asia Minor A. D. 1812. Manuscript copies of his revision are in the library of the British legation at Tehran. A copy was presented to the Shah. Prince Galitzin, the head of the Russian Bible Society, caused an edition of five thousand copies of Martyn's version to be printed at St. Petersburg for circulation in Western Persia.

The Psalter and New Testament, translated by Henry

Martyn, were printed at Calcutta in 1816. The former was reprinted in London in 1824, and the New Testament also, edited by Dr. Lee, in 1827. The New Testament was reprinted in London in 1837. An edition of three thousand copies of the New Testament was printed at Edinburgh to accompany the translation of the Old Testament made by Dr. Glen, then being printed in Edinburgh. The edition published in St. Petersburg in 1815 is said to have been so incorrect that the publication was stopped by the Russian Bible Society. The version of the New Testament made by Henry Martyn is the only one which has been circulated to any extent. The work has many excellences and also many defects. Among the former may be mentioned the evident adherence of the translator to the Greek text and the critical knowledge possessed by him of that text. One of the chief defects is redundance, even more than is found in writings of native Persians. This defect has greatly augmented the size of the volume, as may be known from the fact that while the English version contains about two hundred thousand words, that made by Martyn has over six hundred thousand words. The size of the book has been a serious hindrance to the general circulation of the Scriptures in Persia.

The Rev. William Glen, of the Scottish mission at Astrakhan, completed a version of the Psalms, and in 1826 was employed by the British and Foreign Bible Society to make a translation of the poetical and prophetical books of the Old Testament. At the same time Mirza Jaffir was employed by the same society to produce a version of the historical books of the Old Testament at St. Petersburg, under direction of Dr. Pinkerton and Dr. Lee. The book of Genesis, published in London in 1827, is said to be the only part of Mirza Jaffir's work which has been printed. The books of Psalms and Proverbs, translated by Dr. Glen and revised by Mr. Greenfield and Mr. Selden, were published in London in 1830–31 in an edition of one thousand copies. Another edition was issued in 1836.

In 1847 the entire Old Testament, as translated by Mr. Glen, was printed at Edinburgh. The entire Old Testament was translated by the Rev. T. Robinson of Poonah in India, and completed nine years before the publication of Mr. Glen's version.

In 1834 the British and Foreign Bible Society published an edition of a version of the Psalms made by Mirza Abraham of East India College, Haileybury, and revised by Mr. Johnson of that college. The texts used were the Authorized English version and the Hebrew. In 1842 five thousand copies of Martyn's version of the New Testament were printed by the lithographic process in Calcutta. This was an edition so wretchedly executed as to be unreadable by Persians, and a disgrace to all foreign attempts to print Persian.

In 1844 five thousand copies of Genesis and part of Exodus, as translated by Robinson, were also lithographed. Thus it appears that much was done in the way of preparation of the word in Persian.*

Although these Scriptures have not been so generally circulated as to affect the masses of the people in Persia, yet copies of several of these versions are frequently to be found in the libraries of Persians. The next effort at a version of the New Testament in Persian was made by Rev. Robert Bruce. He had been a missionary of the Church Missionary Society in India, and had some knowledge of the Persian as spoken in that country. He removed to Persia in 1869, and settled in Julfa, near Ispahan, for the purpose of carrying on his translation-work. This was prosecuted in connection with mission-work until the spring of 1881, when the manuscript was sent to the British and Foreign Bible Society for publication. A preliminary examination of the work was made by Professor Palmer of Cambridge and by Rev. James Bassett, then on his return to Tehran. The manuscript was then revised by Mr. Bruce and Professor Palmer, and published for the British and Foreign Bible Society at Leipsic in 1882. The publication was supervised by Mr. Bruce. This version follows, at the discretion of the translator, the text of the Revised Version published in 1881 and the Authorized Version or textus receptus.

* The foregoing statements touching the authorship of these versions are made on the authority of *Bible in All Lands, Hanway*, and the *History of the British and Foreign Bible Society*.

Thus there have been made in the Persian one version of the Pentateuch, two versions of the entire Old Testament, three versions of the whole New Testament and five versions of the four Gospels, besides the versions of the Gospels included in the translations of the entire New Testament. The versions now most used in Persia are Martyn's of the New and Glen's version of the Old Testament.

As a dialect of the Turkish language is spoken by many thousand people of Northern Persia, we ought not to omit some mention of what has been done to give the Scriptures to the Turkish-speaking people of that country.

The missionaries of the Basle society in Southern Georgia translated the New Testament into the Trans-caucasian Tartar. By this name is designated the dialect of the Turkish spoken south of the Caucasus Mountains. The manuscript was long in the possession of the British and Foreign Bible Society. The translation of the Gospel by Matthew in this dialect was printed by that society in 1836. The translation is understood to have been made by Amirchanjanz, an Armenian in the employ of that mission.

In 1872 a version of the Gospel by Matthew in the Azarbijan Turkish was made by Mr. Labaree in Oroomiah for the American Bible Society, and published by him in Leipsic. The term "Azarbijan Turkish" denotes the dialect of the Turkish which is spoken in the province of Azarbijan in Western Persia. It is essentially the same as the dialect called Transcaucasian Tartar. In 1876, Mr. Labaree completed and published for the Bible Society, in Constantinople, a translation of the Gospel by John.

In the mean time, a version of the New Testament in the Transcaucasian Tartar was being made in Tiflis for the British and Foreign Bible Society by Abraham, a son of the above-named Amirchanjanz. Previous to this Abraham was a missionary of the Basle society and was stationed for a time at Tabriz. His work is understood to be a revision of the manuscript prepared by his father. His work was completed in 1878 and published in London.

In 1878–79 a version of the Gospel by Matthew in the Takah Turkmanee was made by Rev. James Bassett in Tehran for the British and Foreign Bible Society. It was published by that society in February, 1880. The translator was aided by a Jew of Mashhad. The version was designed for Turkmans of Ahäl, Merv and North-eastern Persia. The language of these people is a branch of the Turkish known as Gaghatai. All the foregoing versions in Turkish follow the Greek text of the receptus.

No versions of the Scriptures or translations of other books into the Armenian language have been made in Persia, though there are many Armenians in that country and their vernacular is much affected by the Persian tongue.

The Syriac language is used in Persia by the Nestorians only. The history of the Syriac version belongs to the era and country of the Syrian Church, but it will be in place here to note what has been done in Persia in the way of Syriac versions. In 1836, Dr. Perkins began a translation of the New Testament from the Greek text into the vernacular or modern Syriac of the Nestorians. The work was completed in 1846, and published with the ancient version in parallel columns. Immediately on completion of this book Mr. Perkins began a translation of the Old Testament from the Hebrew text into the vernacular of the Nestorians. The New Testament was printed at Oroomiah from type made by Mr. Breath of Oroomiah. This version of the Old Testament was completed in 1852, and thus the whole Bible was given to the people in their vernacular.

The difficulties to be met in making a good translation in the Persian are very great. These are greater in the use of the Persian than of the Turkish. In the latter there is a notable regularity in the formation of all the parts of speech. The vocabulary also need not be supplied from the Arabic. But the Arabic element can hardly be dispensed with in the Persian. It gives much diversity both as to construction and vocabulary. The modern Persian is deficient in the latter element. This deficiency is supplied from the Arabic, and the words used to express religious thought are such terms as the populace do not employ. The conciseness of the Greek and of the Hebrew is poorly represented in the redundance of the Persian, and it is with difficulty that the translation of the Scriptures can be brought into any fair-sized volume. As late as 1872 the only editions of the Old and New Testaments in Persian were octavo volumes of 1658 and 532 pages respectively. The only edition of the whole Bible was, as previously stated, a volume of 2190 octavo pages, which after a great reduction from its cost, could not be sold for less than eight karans, or about one-third or one-fourth of the usual monthly wages of a Persian laborer. This form and size of the Bible were thought to be necessary, owing to the model form of the Arabic letter. The evil has not yet been wholly remedied, yet any one who will observe the small compass into which the Koran is brought, and in which some Persian books are written, will see that reduction is yet practicable. The small volume of the entire Bible which the courteous superintendent of publication of the British and Foreign Bible Society, Rev. William Wright, caused to be printed at the request of the mission in Tehran, is a decided improvement in the way of size, but is only a step in the right direction. The translation itself is verbose, and the printers of England and throughout Europe who use the Persian type do not understand the language so as to make the best use of the type.

In 1880 an edition of the New Testament was printed

for the American Bible Society at the mission-press in Lodiana by the lithographic process. It is a 16mo volume of 920 pages. But the indistinctness caused by printing so closely and in so fine a letter by this process has made the book available to the best readers only.

What has been done in the way of the circulation of the Scriptures in Persia is shown, in part, by the reports of the different missions in that land. All the missions have done something in this line. In fact, it has been a conspicuous part of their labors. These efforts began with the tours of the eccentric Wolff. But, judging from the manner in which he traveled and the length of his journeys, and the state of the countries through which he passed, it seems fair to conclude that he could not at any time have taken any large number of books with him. The efforts of the missionaries of the Basle society and of the American Board were confined to North-western Persia. The latter missionaries were especially concerned with the work in the Syriac language. The earliest missionaries had much to do to prepare the books and the way before the work of distribution could begin. The missionaries of the London Society for Promoting the Gospel amongst the Jews accomplished much, but their work was chiefly with Hebrews. In 1870–71, Bible-distribution was carried on in the vicinity of Ispahan by the agents of Mr. Bruce of Julfa. In 1870 bookstalls were opened in Tehran, Tabriz and Hamadan, and kept by Nestorians under the direction of the missionaries of Oroomiah. These dépôts were not, however, centres of circulation for the country at large nor for the districts in which they were placed. They were designed especially for the work in the cities in which they were located. The opening of the mission in Tehran in 1872 and of Tabriz in 1873 was attended with systematic arrangements for the circulation of the Scriptures throughout the northern half of Persia.

It is an encouraging fact that the Persian government has made no objection to the Bible-work in that kingdom. It has prohibited neither the production of Christian books nor the distribution of these works by sale and gift. The importation of Bibles and other books has not been forbidden.

There is not much to be said of other books than the Bible in the Persian tongue, for the reason that there are but few. So far as any are known in Persia at this time, they are the following, to wit: *Mezon al Haek*, "The Scale of Truth," a work on the Mohammedan controversy, and composed by Rev. Dr. C. G. Pfander, one of the Basle missionaries; *The Key of Mysteries*, a work on the doctrine of the Trinity, also by Pfander; *Keith on Prophecy*, translated by Rev. J. L. Merrick, of the American mission in Oroomiah, in the early years of that mission. A Prayer-book and a Bible history have been prepared by Rev. Robert Bruce of Julfa. Hymns in Persian, *The Tract Primer* and *The Shorter Catechism* have been translated by Rev. James Bassett, and a translation of the first part of Bunyan's *Pilgrim's Progress* has been made by Rev. Joseph L. Potter. In the Turkish of Persia or Azarbijan we have the *Tract Primer*, translated by Rev. J. N. Wright, and a small collection of hymns prepared at first in Oroomiah.

INDEX.

A.

Abasabad, colony of, 327.
Abraham Mirza, 116.
   priest, 111.
   Usta, 241.
Accessions to churches, 72.
Acmetha, 28.
Adultery, 313.
Advance of Russians, 323.
Advantages of Tehran, 100, 311.
   from foreign influence, 313.
Ahmad, a writer, 53.
Aladdin's lamp, 6.
Alcoholic drinks, 55.
Alexander, Dr., 238.
Almood, 27.
Amene Sultan, 250.
American Board, 75.
Ancient cities, 27.
Annual report, 277, 278.
Antiquities, 28.
Apocryphal books, 28.
Apostasy, penalty of, 34, 99.
Appearance of the people, 29.
Appointments, females, 29.
Archbishop, opposition of, 106, 107.
Armenian churches, 86.
   drunkenness, 111.
   exorcists, 40.
   prostitution, 98.
   Russians, 86.
   schools, 86.
   women, 68.
Armenians, objects of labor, 34.
Arsacia, 27.
Arsenic, use of, 56.
Aryans, 27.
Asp Davon, 77.
Assassins, 27.

Astrology, 41.
Aubdar, 110.

B.

Baba, a colporteur, 99, 108, 114.
Babilla, 119, 125, 128.
Baker, Dr., 112.
Baku, mission in, 156, 159.
Baptism of Jews, 203.
Bargashod, 198, 199, 200.
Bartlett, Miss Cora, 239, 262.
Basle, Society of, 113.
Bassett, Rev. James, removal to Tehran, 74–76, 99, 113; goes to Ispahan, 121; journey to Tiflis, 154; obtains orders for Jews, 176; translation-work, 178, 179; at Mashhad, 187; goes to Hamadan, 198; return to America, 209, 210; return to Persia, 220–222; reply to British minister, 227; appeal to Persian minister, 230, 231; supervision of chapel, 245–249; return to America, 268.
   Mrs. A. W., 135.
   Miss Sarah, 163, 234; returns from America, 252; reports girls' school, 277.
Baubes, 51, 173; temper of, 182; tenets of, 182; Ismael, 183.
Beginning of the mission, 99, 100.
Belief, 36.
Benjamin, S. G. W., 248, 249, 279.
Bible, an oracle, 41; distribution of, 125; division of Bible-work, 216–218; fruits of, 297, 298; Bible-work, 321; societies, 322; in Persia, 331–345; size of, 342;

circulation of, 343, 344; and the Persian government, 344.
Bliss, Rev. Dr., 124.
Boghe, Firdose, 132.
Bohmain, village of, 111.
Book of Ezra, 28.
Bookroom, 139.
Books of the Jews, 41, 52, 100; Christian, 124; in the Armenian, 164; kind needed, 298, 299.
Boys' school, 234.
British and Foreign Bible Society in Tiflis, 160; publications of, in Persian, 164; spirit of, 164, 165.
British and Foreign Office, 247.
British legation, 94.
British minister, 212, 213; order of, 213; reply of, 225-228, 247.
Bruce, Rev. Robert, 74, 99; work of, in Julfa, 123; in Hamadan, 177, 215; revision by, 338; works of, in Persian, 344.
Building, difficulties of, 245.

C.

Calcutta edition of the Scriptures, 337.
Captive colonies, 327.
Carepet, 187, 212.
Caspar, 147, 167, 212.
Caspian coast, 26.
sea, 25; experience on, 221.
Casveen, 24, 27; gate, 112.
Catechism, 269, 344.
Cemetery, 235.
Censor of the press, 178.
Chapel in Tehran, 207; closing of, 229, 231, 235, 236.
Chaplaincy for Tehran, 237.
Character of foreigners, 97.
of Mr. Scott, 207.
Characteristics of Persians, 34.
Chess, 57.
Children of Jews, 166, 167.
Christianity and Islam, 295, 296.
Circulation of the Bible, 343.
Cities of antiquity, 27.
of the Bible, 28.
Class of young men, 136.
Closing of the chapel on account of orders, 229.
Coan, Rev. G. W., 121, 122.
Colbrook, Col., version by, 335.
Cold on the plain, 83.
College of the Shah, 98.

College for Persia, 319.
Colony, 89; in Mashhad, 329.
captive, plea for, 327.
Colportage, 124.
Colporteurs, 98; for Yezd, 125, 126; trial of, 127, 171-174.
Concentration of wealth, 313.
Concubinage, 56, 105.
Conditions of grant of land, 236.
Confession of Faith, 169.
Congregations, permanent, 291.
Congress, acts of, relating to Persia, 247, 248.
Construction of chapel, 105, 107.
Contrasts in fields, 25, 26, 27, 31.
Controversial books, 49, 52, 53.
spirit, 50.
Controversy, 52, 53; with mullahs, 286.
the Mohammedan, 298.
Converts, how received, 296.
Mohammedan, 170, 216.
male and female, proportion of, 72, 73.
of Jews in Hamadan, 175-177.
Copy of orders of the authorities, 231.
Costume of the women, 65, 68.
Course of study in schools, 297.
Criticism, 307.
Cruelty of mullahs, 51.
Curing by prayer, 44.
Customs, 90.

D.

Damavand, Mt., 23, 25, 26, 80, 83, 89.
Damgan, city of, 27.
Darooz, village of, 111.
Daüd, Mirza, 193.
Dead, disposal of, 90.
Death of Mr. Scott, 207.
Deception, a trait, 53, 55.
Defence of the faith, 52.
Demoniacal possession, 39.
Departed spirits, superstition concerning, 43.
Departure of Mr. Scott, 207.
Destiny of Persia, 825.
Deves or devils, 37.
Difference in fields, 24.
Difficulties of the field, 301-310, 315-318.
of the translation-work, 341.
Dispersed state of sects, 317.

Disposition of the sects, 94.
Disreputable pursuits, 90.
Division of mission-premises, 223.
Divorces, 171.
Doctrine of succession, 35.
Doctrines, effective, 293, 296.
Dress, 29.
Drunkenness at night, 147.

E.

Easter in school, 276.
Eastern Persian Mission, 23, 344.
Easton, Mr., 113, 121.
Eelkhanah, 203.
Eclipse of the sun, 237.
Educational institutions, 302.
Effect of polygamy, 64.
  of Sheahism, 59.
Elburz Mountains, 24, 83.
Encouragements, 310, 314, 318, 324, 325.
English chapel, effort for, 235, 236, 237.
  service of Church, 182, 249.
Environments of Tehran, 80.
Episodes, 153, 251.
Errors of reports, preface, 8.
Esteem of learning, 48.
Esther, Queen, 28.
European governments, relation of, to Persia, 317.
Europeans, number of, 85.
Evil eye, 38.
  spirits, 38.
Exorcism, 39, 40.
Exploration, success and use of, 322.

F.

Famine in Hamadan, 114.
Farhaud Mirza, 131.
Fatima, 59.
Fattah Ale Shah, 53.
Fears of the Armenians, 107.
Females, appearance of, 29.
Feruzbahrom, village of, 109.
Fictions of the Shah, preface, 5.
Filth of Persia, 30.
First efforts of missionaries, 284.
Flight of colporteurs, 126.
Floods, 114.
Foreigners, character of, 97, 309.
  protection of, 310.

G.

Gambling, 57.
Gardens, 29.
Gate, Casveen, 86.
Ghouls, 37.
Girls' school, 135, 219; report of, 262, 267, 269, 275, 280.
Governor, 140.
Great cities, 27.
Grouping of missions, 23.
Guebers, 90, 93.
Guergues, 119.

H.

Hajah Mullah Ismael, 182, 183.
  Ahmad, 52.
Hamadan, 28, 114–116, 119, 132, 136, 140–153, 174–177, 198, 200, 203, 214–216, 219, 221–224, 232, 246, 250–252, 270–272.
Hawkes, Mr., 224, 232, 252, 270.
Healthfulness, 83.
Heat of Vanah, 112.
Hecatompylos, 27.
Henry Martyn, 50; methods, 282.
History of versions of Scripture, 331–344.
Hosein Ale, 192.
  Khan, 222.
Houses, 29, 114.
Hyim, 176, 203, 216.
Hymns in Persian, 165, 166.

I.

Ignorance of the Persians, 86.
Illness, 209; of missionaries, 222.
Imam Reza, 27.
Imitations in theology, 294, 295.
Influence of the Bible, 297, 298.
  of foreigners, 309, 310.
  social, 326.
Inns, 30.
Instruction of Mohammedans prohibited, 213, 214.
Intelligence, increase of, 319.
Intemperance, 56, 128, 144, 147.
Intercession for natives, 197, 310.
Interview with the governor of Hamadan, 140.
Intolerance, Russian, 159, 160; Persian, 315, 316.
Intoxicating drinks, 55.
Isaac, Theodore, 239.
Ismael, Hajah, 183.

350 INDEX.

J.

Jacob of Tus, 332.
Jan, doctor of Hamadan, 176.
Jessup, Dr. H. H., 248.
Jewesses, disorderly, 166; meetings for, 256.
Jews, superstitions of, 47.
　intemperance of, 56.
　of Tehran, 89, 90, 166.
　persecution of, 167.
　of Hamadan, 175, 176, 202.
　in Tajreesh, 204.
　school for, opened, 166; closed, 212; reopened, 233.
Jewett, Miss Mary, 222.
Jins, superstition concerning, 37.
Journey of colporteurs, 126.
Julfa, 123.

K.

Kalyon, use of, 56.
Karaghan, school opened, 153; opposition, 196, 197.
　visited, 198, 209.
　condition of the people, 198, 201.
　work renewed in, 209.
Karaj, 80.
Karman, 24.
Kashan, 27.
Kashish Khanah, 147.
Kathoda of Shevarin, 143.
Keith on Prophecy, 344.
Keun, secretary of legation, 250.
Key of Mysteries, 344.
Khalafah of Baghdad, 27.
Khorasan, 24; name of, 26.
Kilishkin, village of, 76.
Koran, superstition about, 41, 44.
Kurds, 27.

L.

Labaree, Rev. Benjamin, Jr., 101, 124.
Land, grant for chapel, 236.
　of the Imams, 7, 8.
　of the Sun, 26.
Language, 100; use of Persian, 100, 124.
Lar, village of, 198, 200.
Lazar goes to Rasht, 101, 232, 255.
Learned Persians, 313.
Legation, British, 94, 97, 249.
　of the United States, 246, 247, 249.

Liberty, religious, 99, 143; of Mohammedans, 213.
　precedent of, 320, 321.
Limits of mission-fields, 23.
Liquor traffic, 56.
Literature, Christian, 163, 164, 331, 332.
Lotka, Rev., in Hamadan, 232.

M.

Manner of life of Persians, 31.
Manufacture of liquor, 56, 128.
Marriage, child-, 65.
　of Caspar and Carepet, 212.
　of Mr. Hawkes, 254.
　of Mr. Potter, 204.
Martyn's version, 336.
Mashhad, 27, 187, 193; colony of Jews, 329.
Mashhade Sar, 180, 181.
Matteos, 101, 102.
Mazandaran, 28.
Mechail, 113, 116; goes to Rasht, 177; to Mashhad, 187.
Medical missions, 299, 300.
Megerditch, 110, 111, 112, 178.
Men of wealth, 28.
Merrick's translation of Keith, 344.
Methods of mission-work, 281–300.
　of preaching, 295, 296.
　of aiding the colonies, 328.
Minister, British, 225, 230.
　of Persian Foreign Affairs, 230, 231.
Mission, beginning of, 74; plan of work, 100.
　in Oroomiah, 75.
　in Persia, 75.
Mission-premises, 194–196, 307.
　proposed division of, 223.
Missionaries and the authorities, 172, 197.
　return of, to Persia, 220, 221; and the legation, 310.
Modern cities, 27.
Mohammedans, 85, 93; why not converted, 171.
　colporteur of, 171; and Jews, 203, 204.
　prohibited from attending church, 213.
　received to the Church, 216.
　races, 28; number, 34.
Montgomery, Miss Anna, 239, 251, 254.

INDEX. 351

Moral characteristics, 34.
Mordecai, 28.
Mosques of Tehran, 303.
Mountains, 25.
Mujtaheed of Yezd, 126, 179.
Mullahs, studious, 47; relation to Shah, 94.
  spirit of, 47, 50, 51.
  ignorance of, 49.
Music in worship, 165, 166, 292, 293.
Musicians, release of, 121, 122.
Mustofe, 152.

N.

Naibe Sultan, 106, 107.
Narrative, object of, preface, 9.
Native preachers, 290.
Neavaron, 105.
Necromancy, 40.
Nestorian helpers, 99, 290.
Night-journey to Nobaron, 201.
Night-drinking, 147.
Nobaron, 200.
Northern Persia, 24.
Nurillah, 233.
Nusrat id Deen, 52.

O.

Observances of Sheahs, 35.
Officers of government, 172.
  and missionaries, 172.
Ohanes, 113; of Shevarin, 132.
Opening of mission, 74.
Opium, 56.
Opposition of the archbishop, 106, 109, 140.
Oracale, priest, 151.
Oracle, 41.
Order of Sadr Azam, 173.
  of Mustofe and Shah about taxes, 151, 152.
  about school in Karaghan, 196, 197.
  of Sadr Azam about Jews in Hamadan, 176.
  concerning Mohammedans, 213, 214.
  in behalf of Shamoon, 223.
  prohibiting missionaries, 224–231.
  prohibiting missionaries, effect of, 229.
  copy of, from Persian minister, 231.
Organization of the church in Tehran, 168.
  of the church in Hamadan, 175.

Organization of the church in Rasht, 156, 255.
  of the churches, 323.
  of the Eastern Persian Mission, 239.
Origin of Jewish colony, 89.
Oroomiah, 75.

P.

Parthia, 26, 27.
Peasants, 30.
Permanent missions, 291.
Persecution of Mechail, 114, 116.
  in Tabriz, 121.
  of Protestants, 170.
  in Hamadan, 198, 208, 212, 219, 220, 246, 250, 251.
Persia and Christian lands, 31.
  proper, 27.
Persian mission-fields, 24.
  race, 27.
  Armenians, 86.
Persians, very religious, 34.
Petition of the church in Hamadan, 220.
Pfander's books, 298.
Physicians, native, 89, 209.
Pivotal doctrines, 296.
Plain of Tehran, 80, 83.
Plains, 25.
Plea for captive colonies, 327.
Plots against Sadr Azam, 105, 106.
Poetry, influenced by, 59.
Police, order referred to, 231.
Political preferment, 89.
Polygamy, effect of, 64–66.
  not practiced, 131.
  of church-members, 171.
Porter, Rev. T. J., 268.
Possibilities of Persia, 324.
Postal system, 318.
Potter, Rev. J. L., arrival, 139; goes to Oroomiah, 177; begins translation of *Pilgrim's Progress*, 179; journey of, to Baku, 180, 181; goes to America, 184, 185; marries, 204; removes, 232, 233; work of, 235, 241, 269, 345.
Potteries, 27.
Poverty of the people, 28.
Power of conscience, 285.
Prayer, Mohammedan, 36.
  cure, 44, 148.
Preaching, 136.
  in Persia, 282–300.

352　INDEX.

Precedents of liberty, 320.
Premises, mission, 135; purchased, 194-196.
　mission occupied, 204.
Presbyterian Board of Missions, 75.
Press, printing, 139.
Priest, of Vanak, 110, 111; of Shevarin, 143, 144.
　of Hamadan, 151; of Baku, 159.
　Shamoon of Hamadan, 175.
Prince-governor of Hamadan, 143.
Prohibition of liquor traffic, 55, 56.
Prosody, Persian, 165, 166.
Prostitution, 97, 98.
Protection of missionaries, 94, 235, 247, 248.
　of Persians, 310.
Protestant village, 109, 214, 215.
　colony of Shamakha, 159, 160.
Providential openings, 326.
Public baths, 31.
Publication in Persia, difficulties of, 178.
Purchase of mission-houses, 194-196.
Pursuits, disreputable, 90.

Q.

Queen, 105.
Quarentine, 180, 181.

R.

Ra, 28.
Raghes, 27, 28.
Raheem, 176, 203, 219.
Railways, 324.
Ramazan, 55.
Rasht, 27; work begun, 155; church in, 156, 221.
Readers in Tehran, 312.
Reform in Hamadan, 115.
Reinforcements, 154, 155; detained, 180.
Religious state of the people, 33-57.
　Tract Society, 124.
Removal of Armenians of Feruzbahrom, 108, 109.
Renting houses in Persia, 194.
Reply of the British minister, 225, 227, 228.
　of Mr. Bassett, 227, 228.
Report of 1879, 210.
　of 1880, 217-219.
　of 1882, 240.
　of 1883, 252, 255.
　of 1884, 268-272.

Report of 1884, for Hamadan, 270-272.
　of British Foreign Office about missionaries, 247.
　of woman's work, 255, 280.
　of Miss Bartlett, 262-267.
　of Mrs. Bassett, 255, 256.
　of Mrs. Potter, 256-262.
　of Miss Schenck, 273-277.
　of Miss Sarah Bassett, 277-280.
Representatives, foreign, 94, 304.
Results, promise of, 319.
　present, 319, 324.
Reverence for maternity, 43, 44, 64.
Revival in Feruzbahrom, 107, 108.
　in Hamadan, 115.
　in Tehran, 166, 267, 289.
Revolt, 26.
Reza, Imam, 187-189.
Rich and poor, 30.
Rites of Guebers, 86, 93.
Roman Catholicism and Sheahism, 294, 295.
Romance, 282.
Russian Armenians, 86, 159, 160.
　advance, effect of, 323.
Russians, intolerance of, 159.

S.

Sabbath in Persia, 160.
　services, 106.
Sacred books, 40.
Sadr Azam, 102, 172, 173, 212.
Said Saduk, 53.
　Khan, 222, 246, 250.
Saloons, 56.
Sargis of Shamakha, 159.
Sayeds, 35, 60.
Scale of Truth, 53.
Schenck, Miss Anna, 181, 234.
Scholars, 139.
School, 89; in Shevarin, 132, 136, 139; condition, 239; Guebers, 90, 93, 101; village, 108, 112, 123; city, 128, 296, 297.
Science of dreams, 41, 42.
Scorpions, 27.
Scott, Rev. David, 181, 204, 207.
Scriptures in Persian, 164, 174, 342.
Secular authorities and Olema, 51.
Sef ul Ommah, 52.
Sekah marriage, 66.
Senah, 24.
Servants, 30.
Shah, 63, 84, 85, 94, 102, 230, 231.

INDEX. 353

Shah, grants by, 236, 247, 307.
  petitions to, 152, 208.
Shamakha, 159.
Shamoon, priest, 175; threatened, 219; flees, 222; returns to Hamadan, 223.
Sheahism, 34-36, 59, 294, 316, 317.
Sherwood, Miss, 252.
Shevarin, 113, 140, 143, 144, 250, 251.
Shimron, Mt., 80, 84; ascent, 153, 154.
Shrine of Fatima, 27.
  of Imam Reza, 27.
Shrines, 35.
Smith, Lieut.-Col., 249.
Smokers, 56.
Snowstorm, 76.
Social influence, 326.
Sodomy, 56, 57.
Speculative spirit, 309.
Spies, 106.
Spirit of religious orders, 47.
Spirits, belief in, 36-38, 43.
Stocking, Mr., 163.
Subjects of study of mullahs, 48.
Subscription for chapel, 235, 236.
Success of the mission, 319-324.
  of the Bible-work, 321.
Succession, doctrine of, 35.
Sultaneah, 113.
Summary of statistics, 272.
Summer retreat, 128, 153, 268.
Sun, eclipse of, 237.
Suneeism, 34.
Superhuman beings, 37.
Superstition, 36, 44, 47.
Supervision of girls' school, 135.
Synagogues, Jewish, 89.

T.

Tajreesh, 128, 203, 204.
Takah translation, 209.
Taste of Persians, 303.
Taxes of Armenians, 151.
Tchenoktche, 198.
Teachers of girls' school, 135.
Tears, power of, 44.
Tehran, 23, 24, 27, 75, 80, 84, 94, 212.
Telegraph, 318.
Temptations, 308-310.
Theodore Isaac, 239, 240.
Tiflis, mission-work in, 160.
Tobacco, 56.
Toleration, 56; of Sheah and Sunee, 94.

Torrence, Dr. W. W., 220, 232, 241, 269.
Tours, 75, 323.
Tower of Silence, 90.
Tract Primer, 178, 179.
Transfer of missions, 75; of property, 196.
Treacherous temper of mullahs, 50. '
Trial of mujtaheeds, 51.
  of Baubes, 51.
Turkish races, 27.
Twelve, sect of, 59, 93.

U.

Union of schools, 101.
Use of the Kalyon, 56.

V.

Vanak, 109, 110.
Van Duzee, Miss, 163.
Varomene, 80.
Vartinoff, Avek, of Baku, 156.
Versions of the Scriptures, 332-341.
Vices, 55.
View, 25.
Villages, 29, 107, 108.
Virtue of Armenians, 97.

W.

Wealth, 309, 313.
Western Persian Mission, 23, 25.
Wilson, Mr., 222.
Whipple, Rev. Wm., 216, 217, 322.
Wine, 55.
Wright, Rev. J. N., 345.
  Rev. Wm., 164.
Wolff, Rev. Joseph, 322.
Woman's work for women, 255-267, 273-280, 300.
Women, condition of, 58-73.

Y.

Yangee Kallah, 198.
Yasse Attar, 212.
Yohannan, deacon, 165.
Young men of Persia, 311, 312.

Z.

Zain al Abadeen, 220.
Zambar, village of, 198, 200.

www.ingramcontent.com/pod-product-compliance
Lightning Source LLC
Chambersburg PA
CBHW030259240426
43673CB00040B/1006